S0-BTS-336

It's ABOUT *Time:*

THE DIVINE JOURNEY

YESTERDAY,

TODAY AND

FOREVER

BY

Lisa Patrice Hamil

It's ABOUT Time:
The Divine Journey Yesterday, Today and Forever

Copyright © 2016 by Lisa Patrice Hamil
All rights reserved, including the right to reproduce this book or
portions thereof in any form whatsoever. No part of this publica-
tion may be reproduced, stored in a retrieval system, or transmit-
ted in any form or by any means, electronic, mechanical, pho-
tocopying, recording, scanning or otherwise, without the prior
written permission of the author.

ISBN 13: 978-1540587572
ISBN 10: 1540587576

Scripture quotations taken from the New American Standard Bi-
ble˚(NASB), Copyright © 1960, 1962, 1963, 1968, 1971, 1972,
1973, 1975, 1977, 1995 by The Lockman Foundation. Used by
permission. www.Lockman.org

Printed in the United States of America.

Lisa Patrice Hamil
P. O. Box 2391
Santa Cruz, California 95063

Lisa@Creatingyourjoy.com
408-239-7315

ABOUT LISA HAMIL

Lisa has a deep appreciation of God and His Creation. She is inclined to enjoy nature by walking and driving throughout the country just to experience the wonder of such beauty.

Her education includes a Doctor of Pharmacy, Real Estate Broker, Masters in Business Administration, Doctor of Ministry and Certified Professional Coach.

She is a speaker, author, singer, songwriter, and producer of musical productions, business owner, pharmacist and minister. She believes her mission is to share the teachings and reality of God through biblical understanding.

Lisa is a proponent of lifestyle and health that has a significant foundation in faith for vibrant wellbeing. She thrives in the grace and joy of our Creator daily.

How thoughts manifest reality and managing judgment are her pillars for building a life of gratitude and thanksgiving. She believes these are the tools for creating your joy.

TESTIMONIALS

FOR

It's ABOUT *Time:* THE DIVINE JOURNEY YESTERDAY, TODAY AND FOREVER

Lisa has a very special gift to translate into plain words the most intricate spiritual teachings.

If you want to have a breakthrough and find more peace, joy and happiness the truth is that none of those will be found on the outside world.

With Lisa's help you will be able to navigate the sometimes difficult waters of spirituality in an easy way so you can bring those teachings into your everyday life to experience the joy that we are all searching for.

With much love and appreciation for your work, Lisa.

–Erika Ferenczi

An excellent dissertation on how valuable time is and on how little many of us value it.

Time is our friend: "Time heals all wounds." Time is our enemy. "The time has come and now is." Time is fleeting. "You know not the time or the hour."

We cannot create time. The Lord has done that and has allotted some to each of us. How we use it is more important than how much we have. Sadly, this is a lesson many of us learn late in life.

I commend Lisa Hamil on her work. She made me think about it, and at my age that's not really something I want to do. To put things in some perspective, have you ever heard a dying man say, "I wish I had spent more time at the office"?

–Bud Photopulos

Your book was a lovely read. The discussion and analysis of time really drew me in. I loved that idea of time travel at the speed of thought.

I also enjoyed your stories, especially the one about finding the red shoes and the one about your nightmare of being home when you were in South America. Amazing moment and amazing dream!

–Jamie Gifford

ACKNOWLEDGMENTS

Writing a book is one of life's most revealing experiences of self and *time*.

I cannot take credit for being motivated to relate this information as I am so inspired by God Himself. I am continually amazed at how He shows up in the most unpredictable and compelling circumstances. In this way, I thank Him for His faithfulness in my life and how I see Him working in the world.

I am so grateful for the guidance and filtering of ideas made possible by the proficient readership of Donna Kozik. She allowed me to put concepts together on paper only my mind would understand but not articulate.

My writing career is meager when seen in the light of my inspiring and encouraging colleagues that spur me on with their groundbreaking accomplishments and publications. Among those in my writing groups are Karen O'Connor, Laura Bennet, Carol Nicolet Loewen and Pat Davis who have encouraged me in moving forward with my goals.

Technical writing tips were sought from and graciously provided by Sue Wolbach, Laura Bennet, Carol Nicolet Loewen, Colombo Lisa Smith, Terra Hagan, Pat Davis and Leslie Purtz.

Fr. Tom Paris validated the notes of worthiness and messaging, for which I am encouraged in receiving. Bud Photopolos, Judy and Hugh Seagreaves, were helpful in providing feedback and I much appreciated their considerations, input and impressions.

Joanne Cameron brought the poem, *Doing Time*, to my attention.

I am grateful for the evaluations of impact that were submitted by William Cellona and other readers too numerous to list. Thank you all for relating how this writing touched your heart.

My working title was motivational but not good marketing material. My goals would have never been achieved if it were not for the inspiring suggestion of Phil and Jan Enloe.

I have a tremendous appreciation for the many advocates of learning and relating the Word of God, without which I may very well have not learned to appreciate the magnitude of how much God impacts our time on earth.

DEDICATION

This book is dedicated to one of my significant godmothers,

Joy Nelson
1928–2016

who launched my quest in the reality of God by asking …

"God, if you are, I want to know YOU."

Her birthday was December 3 and I am reminded of the inspirational verse of Daniel 12:3 which says, "And those who have insight will shine brightly like the brightness of the expanse of heaven, and those who lead the many to righteousness, like the stars forever and ever."

She has been that bright star to many.

CONTENTS

INTRODUCTION

How far is it to Miami? How far is it to...?

I am a national park junkie. Having lived in California for most of my life, I took several opportunities for trips to the western national parks; however, I really wanted to experience the national parks in the eastern part of the continental United States. To do this I embarked on an extensive trip from Santa Cruz to Bangor, Maine, and back home.

Acadia National Park on the eastern sea coast of Maine was my furthest destination. I had already driven thousands of miles in getting to Acadia and I could not ignore a consistent perspective on *time*. Without exception, east or west, night or day, police, park ranger or lay person... whenever I would ask, "How *far* is it to 'thus and so?'" the unanimous response was in terms of *time*. "Three hours." "About twenty minutes down this road." "It will take at least a day and a half." These were examples of how my quest for distance or "How far is it to...?" would get answered. You might note how people answer this question of distance for you.

The responses were kind and well intentioned, however, I was on vacation and did not have a significant deadline or appointment to meet. As an example, it might take me two hours to drive 20 miles because I would stop and take pictures, get gas or supplies at a local grocery store or stop to just breathe in the fresh air. Many times I would be walking, and I needed to know how far to plan in the enjoyment of my journey. I became aware of the unusual concept of *time* that people had throughout the country. Distance, to them, was defined by *time*.

This correlation of time and distance crept into my thoughts for several months following that journey. I am by no means an expert, however, how time is allowed to bind us up, and how God's synchronicities play out could not be ignored. This writing reflects some of the perspectives on time and how one might use those perspectives to greater advantage. Even more importantly is how one might be released from *the bondage of time* and just enjoy the moments as they come.

How your thoughts impact the availability of time for you to be what God intended you to be and do, is the focus of this book. You were created, as it says in Ephesians 2:10, as His workmanship in Christ Jesus for good works, which God prepared beforehand, that you should walk in them. The parameters of physical time were established on the fourth day of creation, as stated in Genesis 1:14–19 and provide the basis of our earthly time.

This book is intended to be the first of a six part series that covers *how the six days of Creation can transform the journey of life*. It is a foundational book of considerations regarding personal time and how your relationship to time impacts your journey through life and beyond. If you would like to discuss these topics in more detail, you may reach me at

Lisa@CreatingYOURJoy.com.

This is the Cadillac Mountain of Acadia National Park on the eastern seacoast of Maine. This mountain was named after Antoine de la Mothe Cadillac, who founded Detroit, Michigan. He is the eponym for the luxury vehicle known as the Cadillac. The Cadillac crest is based on his coat of arms. This is one of the few places in the world where granite rock is "pink".

It reminds me of MaryKay every time-Pink Cadillac promo cars.

Chapter One

The Current Concept of TIME

I live in a town called Santa Cruz,
Whose name means Holy Cross.
Each day I know I cannot lose,
'Cause He redeems my loss...

Why do people want to be the first person at the stoplight?

Time to Get Going

When I left Santa Cruz for the eastern seacoast of Maine on that June morning, I was backing out of the driveway with my 2002 Kia Sedona van. It already had 211,000 miles on it and I had reliably taken this vehicle to numerous national parks the year before. Everything was now set to visit 20 national parks on this trip. Most of them were east of the Mississippi.

I was to join in on two conferences in New Jersey and pick someone up at the airport before one of them. My plans included time to see several friends in remote cities on the east coast and then sing in churches at every opportunity along the way. I had even scheduled a voice lesson in New York City, since I would be in the neighborhood. Just the Holy Spirit and I were setting out on this 66-day excursion of God's Creation. I was so ready.

My anticipation was met with a most unusual short circuit. As I was leaving, the electrical windows slid open as though they had a mind of their own. Who or what was pushing those power window buttons? A mile and a half later, I was in the repair shop of my favorite mechanic to evaluate the situation. "Power arm-rest bar is gone" was the reply and they had to order the part. No problem. It would be available and replaceable the next day.

Yes, there was a *time* delay of my trip plans, but I knew there had to be a reason. I called to cancel my stay near Fresno with a former working colleague. That was Tuesday morning.

Wednesday morning, I went to the dealership to pick up the Kia plug-in power bar for the driver-side armrest. It was replaced with ease at the repair shop, and off I went on the official first day of my trip across the country. Thank goodness, at this point, I had some flexibility in scheduling and I began anticipating a visit that night with my other friends in Victorville, California.

Three hours into my journey and heading down Interstate Five at about 70 miles per hour, my windshield wipers began to sweep across the glass. A little surprised at this automatic switch in wiper activity, I did what I could to turn them off. It was over 100 degrees outside, my windshield was loaded with insects and the dry rub of the wipers was vexing. I pushed numerous buttons to disengage the wipers and they finally stopped when I turned on the air conditioner. Well, fine.

I really did not want the air conditioner on, so I turned it off. Immediately, the wiper blades raged into high gear, as though they were offended for being turned off in the first place. Their speed was so intense, it seemed as though the van could have launched into space. In less than a minute, a loud explosion sounded and every light on the dashboard disappeared. The wipers stopped wiping and the engine was gone. I was still going at a remarkable speed in the fast lane and had no electrical signals. With incredible *timing*, there was just enough room for me to coast off of the road.

"Great start to a well-planned trip," I thought. It was three in the afternoon and I had plenty of time to call roadside assistance. It would be an hour's wait they said. I was 20 miles north of Bakersfield; it was at least 110 degrees outside, not a tree in sight and no place to charge my phone.

The tow truck driver was great at getting me to his favorite, reliable and trustworthy mechanic. Since I could charge my phone in his truck, I contacted my friends in Victorville to let them know I would probably be late, due to the current events. I also called the mechanic to see what the chances were of getting things taken care of that afternoon so I could be on my way. Time was getting pretty important to me now.

Dropping the van off at the mechanic's shop, I was told that there was a reasonable motel across the street. That did not seem necessary at first; however, after an hour of playing around with the burnt out fuses, replacing the bulging battery and attempting unsuccessfully to get the seven computers to speak to each other, driving on that night was just not going to happen.

I let my friends know I would not make it to their home that night. They strongly recommended that I dump the van and just go home. In their mind, driving all of those miles and days in a vehicle with 211,000 plus miles on it was just unwise. That was a night of serious deliberation.

I could not go home. There had to be another solution. I absolutely could not give up on all of the scheduled events, people I wanted to see and singing that I was planning on doing. I simply prayed for wisdom and went to sleep.

The next morning, I thought I had a semi-brilliant idea. Rent a car! The mechanic had had a technician come in with a better handle on car computers. He also called the Kia dealership down the street for recommendations. Neither party had much to offer at that point. What seemed clear to me was to leave the van at the shop and rent a newer vehicle so I could get going. It took a few hours to transfer belongings to the rental and I was finally on my way.

> *The mind of man plans his way, but the Lord directs his steps.*
> (*New American Standard Bible*, Proverbs 16:9)

That was a serious driving day and I ended up changing a few reservations to make up for lost *time*. Having a rental car seemed to be the perfect solution because not only was there less mileage on the vehicle, but should there be any performance issues, I would have national access to dealerships across the country. I was no longer living in the fear of lost time due to mechanical failures and vehicle unreliability.

Time Today

The universal modern day unit of time is the *second*. What people do with it is based on cultural norms that have been established over the years. The *second* has no time zone. The second is universally *now*. If we were to have a worldwide meeting that happened at exactly "now" we would be engaging in an activity that is happening simultaneously and at the same time. We would not be concerned with time zones.

Galileo paved the way to greater divisions in measuring minutes and hours of time by studying characteristics of the pendulum in the 1500s. Not long afterwards owning a hand-held timepiece was considered a status symbol, they were so costly to produce.

The clocks that emerged from his initial studies became replaced over the years by efficient and economical productions of clocks and watches. More recently, digital timepieces have dominated the tracking of minutes and seconds such that in our age of technology each second is now based on atomic time. Instead of the pendulum's vibration of Galileo's time, it is the energy and vibration of atomic particles that define the passage of time, and the division even of seconds.

Time zones, on the other hand, very from place to place in our world of living. There are 24 time zones established for regional events of legal, commercial and social purposes. The basis of our worldwide time zones is determined from the Royal Observatory of Greenwich, in Greenwich, London. Iceland, however, is located directly south of Greenland and has agreed to use a time frame that is one hour different from the official GMT (Greenwich Mean Time) of Greenland. Further, certain areas of the United States and other areas of the world make special arrangements for taking advantage of daylight savings time. If one looks at a political map of time zones, there is a significant part of the world operating under a gap that exists between official time and solar time. All of these time zone aspects point to the fact that the time in certain areas is brought about by agreement. It is not absolute.

Perspectives on Time

Aside from time zones, time has a cultural component. Years ago, in my graduate training of international marketing, my instructor related his challenges with cultural time. He was sent to South America to improve operations of an American bank.

In our country, when a bank opens for business at 10 a.m., it means that the employees are there and ready for business services at 10 a.m. Not so in this country's cultural practices. When he set up his branch to open at 10 a.m., employees began to trickle in somewhere between 10 and 11 a.m. Sometimes they would come with their friends and catch up on relational conversation.

An eye-opening experience regarding cultural time was when his bank manager showed up to work and how *he* used his time. After an hour or so of doing some of his banking admin-istration, his mistress would come in to continue some of their personal discussions. Not long afterwards, his wife and several children would also come in and the whole group, wife, mistress and children, would enjoy each other's company, laughing and responding to each other's comments. This was their understand-ing of time at work. Needless to say, it was also one of the rea-sons why my instructor had been sent down to South America. He needed to reorient this branch on how they were to work and use their employment time towards company goals based on American corporate standards.

In having traveled to many third world countries, I have seen that a simpler life has its advantages. There is less to take care of, more cooperative group efforts and time for relationship. What seems to matter most is time together as a community.

Establishing the value of time is vital in our day-to-day lives. Of what significance

is the use of time to measure performance? Examples would include the following: in medicine we evaluate a patient's heart beats or breaths per minute; in driving, the measure of miles per hour; in sports, miles run per minute or time left in an inning. Musically, time establishes the rhythm, mood and basis for har-mony and instrumentation. The rate, speed or tempo established with time, serves in the scope of vitality, performance and in get-ting things done with community.

We want to enjoy more *free* time and to do things sooner. We want free time for events, appointments or other important things that *need* to be done. Completing tasks may be more efficient if additional resources and teamwork are used. Lack of cooperation and discipline amongst us with others is *time*-consuming.

With regards to health, being rushed to accomplish a task in a limited amount of time is stressful and often results in anxiety. Reducing food preparation time may not be as healthy as taking the time to build a fresh meal from scratch.

The *speed* factor is part of our daily conversations. There is often something to say about *rush* hour traffic, how time *flies,* and deadlines, just to name a few. Saving time has its rewards as with *instant* gratification, *fast* food, and taking the *fast* track. We may think that we are getting better at managing time; however, it is the result that counts.

Managing Time

Actually, time cannot be managed. Time is always moving no matter what one may think. When things are pleasantly going along, time *flies* because it is *fun.* Events that are unpleasant or boring result in a sense that time is moving very slowly. As long as the earth is rotating, time cannot be held back. What gets done with the available time is all that can be influenced by human beings. A life span on this earth is a measure of time represented most frequently by what is accomplished in those years, and is finite.

In his address to the Stanford graduates several years ago, Steve Jobs said, "Live every day as if it is your last—someday you will be right."

The use of time effectively is where there is room for greater proficiency. Some of the most significant time robbers are negative feelings that clog the flow of creativity and enjoyment. Negative feelings are often associated with judgments that lead to fear. A shortfall in mechanical and performance factors, faulty organization in finding things and emotional disturbances all prolong the time needed to accomplish a task or goal. This was especially true in relation to my trip across the country as related above.

How Fear Affects Your Vitality

In the state of immediate fear, one of the physiologic responses is the release of adrenalin. Adrenalin is considered the "fight or flight" hormone and is characterized by an increase in heart rate, rapid breathing, intense focus on the immediate surroundings, *fight,* or muscular engagement to escape the immediate surroundings, *flight.* This makes sense when real danger is apparent, however, the use of judgment may actually escalate the intensity of fear, when immediate danger is not present.

Smoldering fears that are not associated with an immediate event, are what really impact time. These fears trigger the release of cortisone, often referred to as the "stress" hormone. Stress begins to show up as worry, blame, anger, regret, indecision and a host of other negative emotions. When these emotions begin to take over your thinking, it is difficult to be efficient, and a lot of time is wasted being stuck in unproductive processing. Over a period of time these negative thoughts impair your sleep and impact healthy living. They can cause you to develop high blood pressure, elevated cholesterol, diabetes, psoriasis and a host of other illnesses that reduce your quality of life and ultimately shorten your lifetime.

In my position as a pharmacist, I have seen situations where people had begun a new business or had moved due to job relocations and significant fears began to creep in. Their new responsibilities and stress over financial needs resulted in the development of immune based diseases such as psoriasis, fibromyalgia or multiple sclerosis. Stress due to added responsibilities resulted in increased blood pressure and elevated cholesterol. If left unchecked, in situations like these serious consequences may result, including a debilitating stroke or heart attack. Statistics show that 55 million people die from heart disease worldwide, and 610,000 die of heart disease each year in the United States alone.

If you look at what upsets people the most and how they get involved with complaining and discontent, there is a root of judgment and comparison. This milling around of the mind does not solve any problems, however, it delays the solution of living in the joy of not having the problem. Negative thoughts and emotions contribute significantly to the 832,000 divorces in the United States annually. This negativity also results in two billion people struggling with alcoholism worldwide. A mindset of judgment is what stands in the way of enjoying your life and negative thinking is not time well spent.

Doubting the Possible

Here is an example. Sally was so excited after the first date that she had with Tony. She really thought that he had enjoyed his time with her, as well. When he did not call or text her over the next two days, she began to worry. She made assumptions that he wanted to avoid seeing her. She was stewing over everything that had happened during their time together a few days before.

She was beginning to wonder if she really was good enough to be in a relationship that she enjoyed. Finally, after several days of waiting and out of a fear of rejection, she sent a text to Tony saying that she was tied up with some new and unexpected responsibilities and that she would not be available to see to him for some time.

Several years later, they ran into each other at a local business event. At that point, Sally was married, however, Tony was still single. As they shared what was going on in each other's lives, Sally learned that her text to Tony years ago was devastating to him. He had felt so motivated in pursuing a relationship with her that he wanted to complete another relationship with integrity as well as restore some family connections. He was so focused on doing what he felt he needed to complete, that he delayed contacting her until he was in a better emotional place.

The above example shows how time was wasted when spent judging, feeling judged or incomplete. These negative thoughts were followed by time feeling rejection on both sides of the relationship. In this example, both individuals were living in the position of the *victim*. Each person allowed his or her perception of judgment to overshadow reality. They were afraid to learn the truth before making a significant decision. Can you see that a lot of time was wasted or lost due to unmet expectations, assumptions, interpretations, or negative self-evaluation? Neither side knew the truth. This is not how we were meant to live. We were meant to live a life in love, meaningful connection and joy. It takes courage to believe in and seek the truth in personal relationships.

A joy-filled life may unfold by taking responsibility for how you spend your thinking time. I like to think of responsibility as choosing to use your *ability* to *respond*. The key is to choose versus react. If you are thinking thoughts of rejection, not being good enough, not deserving, or some variation of these, that is what you get. As things begin to unfold in life, God gives you a choice in how you respond. Choosing to be defined by your doubts and the perceived thoughts of others is operating with a victim mentality. God has a better plan in store for you. You are His creation and

He calls you "beloved." Trust Him for the courage that you need in seeking the truth and set yourself up for the best outcome.

Believing in the Possible

Take a look at what David from the Old Testament did. David was slight of stature, considered the weakest of his male siblings. His seven older brothers were the strong and mighty ones that would go off to war, while David was left home tending sheep. As a shepherd, he had to ward off the lion and the bear to protect his flock. His success in warding off predatory animals from the sheep gave him confidence. David was also a musician, playing the harp to delight King Saul, who suffered from evil thoughts and torment. David knew he had the capability of being successful in service.

The Philistines were mighty in size and were threatening the tribe of Israel under King Saul. The Philistine giants intimidated David's three older brothers. They considered David too weak and inexperienced to contend with the warriors. Even King Saul questioned the prudence of having David fight the giant, Goliath. David was determined, knowing that he had been successful in protecting the flock of sheep from the lion and the bear. David was looked upon as but a youth, while Goliath was of mighty stature and strength and had had many successes in battle.

David's thoughts and determination saw him through to success. The rewards were impressive and included the King's daughter for a wife, riches for himself and his family. David was focused on God's power through him, and made short work of the threats represented by the tribe of Philistine warriors. They fled immediately after the giant Goliath was slain by David. The complete story is available in 1Samuel 17. David was living in the way of the *victor.*

This is but one example of how your thoughts impact your success and ultimately allow you to reap the benefits of time well spent. Focusing on the dream result and vision is the secret. Surely, there will be challenges along the way; however, they serve to strengthen your faith, resolve and confidence in your determination. How many Goliaths will you overcome with the vision of success in your lifetime?

The Speed of Thought

If you were sitting in a front row seat of a sold-out Broadway theatre and you needed to leave in a hurry, how long would it take for you to get to the back exit? Getting up from your seat and then walking, or running, to the exit would take several minutes. It could take even longer to leave if the theatre was full of other audience members who wanted to leave also.

In your mind, however, you could be at that exit in just a few seconds. If you are sitting in your living room, the thought of your front door comes to you much faster than you can get up and walk to that door. Your mind's thoughts can travel over distances at a speed comparable to the speed of light. How quickly do you see a dark room light up once you turn on the switch? Your mind's thoughts travel just as fast. If you have traveled to distant parts of the world, and know what it looks like to be there, your thoughts will have taken you thousands of miles to bring that memory back to you in seconds. Your thoughts are powerfully fast over distances.

Why is this important? Several years ago, I was working the night shift in pharmacies all over northern California. The shift usually began at 9:30 or 10 p.m. depending on the store and lasted for ten hours. One night, I was leaving my home to drive to a pharmacy "over the hill" from Santa Cruz to a city some forty miles away. It was raining profusely. There was bumper-to-bumper traffic and I could barely see to drive. Plus, I had concerns regarding the safety of the neighborhood that the pharmacy was in. I was running late and dreading the next 12 hours of my life.

I allowed these circumstances to stress me out. My shoulders and chest were tense. I had a headache. My mouth was dry and my stomach was cramped with tension. The traffic was so backed up no one was going anywhere. In the confining flow of traffic, I turned on my CD player and instantly, all of my tensions were gone. I could not believe the transition of physical symptoms.

What I had tuned into was an oratorio of *The Third Day of Genesis Chapter One, Day of Land, Sea and Vegetation*. The words of the music had been set to a video I had seen previously. The opening line of music brought to mind that video and visions of a shoreline and beach near my home. Transferring my thoughts from the immediate perception of stress and turmoil to the soothing peace of a gentle surf roaming through the sand, completely transformed the tensions of my life in that moment. It was magical.

This experience demonstrated to me the power and speed of thought from the stress of the moment to the relaxing impressions evoked by remembering the pictorial representation of the music. These thoughts were instantly able to transform my physical feelings and symptoms from tension to relaxation and joy.

Have you ever opened up a letter to read of bad news? How did you feel? What would have happened if your next piece of mail were an inheritance check for a generous sum? Thoughts have a powerful impact on your physiology and health and they work quickly.

Summary of Steps to Release Stress with the Speed of Thought

1. Notice thoughts of turmoil.

2. Notice tension in the body; headache, muscle, or abdominal cramping.

3. Notice the label of judgment; anxiety, fear, resentment.

4. Choose a different thought; a loving friend, child, fun activity, a scene of nature.

5. Notice commitment to that thought without reverting back to the first thought #1.

6. Notice release or surrender of tension. Strength of faith is powerful here.

7. Notice feelings of relaxation in the body; relief of headache, or cramping.

The biggest challenge is maintaining the new thought of choice in favor of the thoughts that brought on the stress. A picture of a loved one, inspirational reading, music, scenes of beauty or even a phone call to an up-beat friend will help divert thoughts that bring on stress. It is a practice that strengthens over *time* and is well worth the development.

Doing Time

The prisoner sat alone in thought of his vacated cell
Begging his God to end his time of solitary hell.
Oh, such a waste, to have cut off his days known as his prime.
The act was but a fleeting thought, so small a human crime.

He yearned to know his freedom, the sunshine and the flowers,
And have someone to be with, to fill up all his hours.
But there was now no hope in sight, his life was all but through.
When there onto his windowpane, a gentle sparrow flew.

"Ah, little friend," he said now and, "I envy your life so,
To choose each time with freedom, the way your life will go."
The sparrow stared so blankly there, still perched upon the ledge,
His fearful eyeing of the feline now hid beneath the hedge.

"Ah," said the sparrow then in fear, his voice so filled with grief,
"I may as well be just like you or bonded as a thief.
For though I am considered good and not committed crime,
We, in our own way, live in thoughts of bondage *doing time*."

Adapted from a poem by an Unknown Author

When people read this poem, different messages are derived depending on where that person has been and where they are intending to go. The main point, however, is that physical restraints are real such as prison, trapped under a pile of wood and stone after an earthquake or confined to a hospital bed because of serious surgeries. What people do not realize is that their thoughts keep them just as immobilized, even though there are no physical restraints. They think that self-expression and their surroundings will limit them, so they do not act.

Abraham Lincoln once said, "Always bear in mind that your own resolution to succeed is more important than any one thing."

William Shakespeare offers, "There is nothing either good or bad, but thinking makes it so." From Betty Sachelli, "Two thoughts cannot occupy the mind at the same time, so the choice is ours as to whether our thoughts will be constructive or destructive." And from Napoleon Hill, "Every man is what he is because of the dominating thoughts which he permits to occupy his mind." This last quote is affirmed from Proverbs 23:7, "For as he thinks within himself, so he is…"

Living in the bondage of your thoughts of stress and anxiety leads to physical deterioration and depression. The truth of freedom from that bondage can be found in Galatians 5:1 where it says, "It was for freedom that Christ set us free; therefore keep standing firm and do not be subject again to a yoke of slavery." The discipline of thought in the possible as opposed to the impossible is what can ultimately provide your time of joy. How have your thoughts imprisoned you?

The Value of Time

Time is valuable and it is often said that time is money. There is some truth to this, however, how many people have passed on with a huge bank account and yet were unable to *buy* more time. Time is money *plus* something that could be considered irreplaceable. Money is replaceable. In order to make money, we must have the time to implement an idea or activity in exchange for what someone is willing to pay for it. Perhaps a better analogy would be to say that time is money plus energy, or vitality.

Like most children, I wanted attention and time with my parents. I was an only child for almost six years and I had gotten pretty accustomed to garnering the focus of both my mother and father. After having lived in Austria for over three years and settling in California, my parents began adding additional members to the family. I was a little disturbed when I had to share my mother's time and attention with the other five children that came along over the years. Finally, at the age of thirteen, I had had enough.

I thought to myself that since my mother had five additional children, she would not have that much time for me. Perhaps I could find five other "mothers" to help me with the educational and supportive time that I felt I needed. All of these "mothers" were from 17 to 20 years older than I and somehow, they began to treat me as their daughter. All of them were wise women of faith, as was my own mother, and I learned a lot about God from them.

Consequently, I referred to them as my "godmothers." This proved beneficial in getting the time I felt that I needed to learn what my biologic mother simply did not have time to teach me. All of my "mothers" gave me the value of their time, which translated into enhanced prosperity and improved vitality for me.

Resources Over Time

An additional perspective of time that is relevant to this review is time in relation to population and resources. In the first century of time, 100 A.D., there were 200 million people on the earth. There were 300 million people on the earth by the 10th century. By the 19th century, there were one billion people living on the earth and now, in the 21st century, there are in excess of seven billion people. It is estimated that by the year 2100 or the 22nd century, there will be eleven billion people. Time and experiences over time are teaching lessons for success in survival, health, travel and provisions. The communication of information over time is leading to geometric growth in populations.

It is estimated that if everyone in the world lived as close to each other as the average neighbor, they could all fit in the state of

Texas. Currently, Texas has far more land than people. However, in order to supply all of those people with the material goods that we are accustomed to as Americans, we would need the equivalent landmass of four earths. How many "things" do people really need in order to enjoy their *time* on earth? Our *time* in this country, as a relatively young country, has led to greater material goods and significant prosperity, yet we are seeing less and less true happiness, health and joy.

Time at a Certain Age

Time is also a variable concept. This is especially relevant with regards to age. You have seen grown adults act like children. Yet, some children are wise beyond their years. Children are like sponges in learning new things because they have not yet learned the worldly standards of judgment. They can be brutally honest. Bless them. They also live in the moment. Cheerful objects and attention easily divert a saddened child. They tend not to dwell in those feelings of sadness unless accompanied by dire abuse or trauma. This is a quality of authenticity and vulnerability that is endearing.

Would that adults could adopt more of these childlike characteristics. Holding on to the past is not only harmful to your well-being, it contributes to the bondage of time described in Chapter Four, Time Robbers. Those who have advanced in years must realize that you will never be younger than you are today, so please, enjoy your youth!

Additionally, when working at a scheduled job, people finish their work and do all sorts of things that are necessary to enhance their lifestyle, tend to the garden, family and pets. People that are able to accomplish a lot from day to day have learned to maximize the use of their time. This is a mastered skill. Everyone gets the same 24 hours in a day, yet some get more done during those hours. Busy people have learned how to use time to their advantage. They accomplish doing more because of proficiency with this skill.

Interestingly, once some people retire, all of a sudden they have no time to do anything and wonder how they ever held down a job. Is it because now there are so many new choices? Is it because they have different priorities? Or, is it that they want to slow down a bit? Lots of reasons are possible. Our family joke is, if you want to have something done, do not ask a retired person because they have no time.

At this writing, Lisa Patrice Hamil is 34 years old. However, the author is twice this age because I changed my name in 1982.

I was born in Sofia, Bulgaria, and my given name was Draga Staykoff, in honor of my paternal grandmother, Draga. Moving to America after World War II, our family name became Staykow. During all of my school years, Draga was a difficult name for people to remember correctly, spell or pronounce. After marriage, I became Draga Malaznik and people thought that I had "jumped out of the frying pan into the fire." When that marriage was no longer viable, I thought that it was a perfect time to change my name, altogether. I needed a name that would be easier to pronounce and did not need explaining, thus it had to save *time* for everyone, including myself.

I started out with Elizabeth. Elizabeth was the name that I chose to name myself when going through the American citizenship process. It was my favorite name as an eight-year-old because Elizabeth Taylor was my favorite actress and Queen Elizabeth of England was quite popular at the time. Driving to work on the morning that I changed my name, I drove under the Hamilton Avenue exit sign on the freeway, and I had an instant phonetic epiphany, "Elizabeth Hamilton." That was it! Then, as I was enamored with dance and singing at the time, I threw in Patrice as a middle name, from the entertainer Patrice Muncel.

My new life was starting out with a new name, Elizabeth Patrice Hamilton. However, in the interest of *time,* I shortened this name to Lisa P. Hamil, as otherwise it would have taken forever for me to sign my name. Three months later, this name was legal in the court system. My lawyer said that people *should* change their name every 20 years because they become different people over *time.*

Although chronologically a number of years and experiences have taken place during the past 68 years, it is held with great anticipation that the best is yet to come and life is just beginning to take off. Psychologically, age becomes a function of energy, outlook, anticipation and purpose as well as *time.* Philosophically, the two most important days in your life are the day that you are born and the day that you discover why.

Use of Time Effectively

Over the years, I have discovered the truth of staying centered in John 15:5 where Jesus says, "I am the vine, you are the branches; he who abides in Me, and I in him, he bears much fruit; for apart from Me you can do nothing." So many events of my life are related to reaching some creative goal. Reading and contemplating the words of wisdom and peace from God's Word has cleared the runway to activities I never thought possible on my own.

Delays and redoing seem so much less time-consuming when graced by the blessings available from abiding in the presence of *divine direction.* I am convinced that there is no better way to live than to enjoy the beauty of Mother Nature, the first Bible I knew of as a child, and Father Time, God in His printed Word.

Letting things happen through surrender and listening for direction is the goal. These practices require new habits. Clarity begins by asking in prayer, seeking and then acting on the direction given as Luke 11:9 describes. When a new step is taken, greater clarity for the next step reveals itself. This is the process of building the faith for your *time*.

* * * * * * *

Time is neither an event nor a thing that is measurable. Nor can time be traveled, except in your thoughts. All of these aspects of time point to how closely time is related to perspectives. Growth over time is not linear but geometric. Conversely, deterioration is also geometric. The more time-saving devices and concepts that are available, it appears that less time is available to do what is now important. Given the choice, is it time or things, including money, that are most important? Are you living your lifetime as a human being or a human doing? Is there room for a balance of both? Is there a limitation to your joy because you have adopted a *bondage* to time?

Chapter Two

The Biblical Concept of TIME

God brought me to this place on earth
To live His perfect will
How could I be so fortunate?
My heart with joy to fill

No matter where I go or who I am with, there is one common denominator, ME!

It is fascinating to review the Biblical concept of time and how the terminology differs from the world today. There is no such thing as a *second* in the Bible as a unit of time. There were no devices to measure a second as a unit representing one-sixtieth of a minute. The only time the word *second* is used, is in reference to what comes after the first, such as the *second* coming of Jesus or as in Genesis chapter one, where what happened on the *second* day of creation is described.

In looking at the various words for *time* in the Bible, I discovered that one of the most frequently used words was the word *day*, a total of 2047 times, based on the New American Standard translation. However, that was not the most frequently used word for time, to my surprise. Please see the table at the end of this chapter.

Can you imagine what the most frequently used word for a unit of time might have been in Biblical writings? It is the word *now*. The word *now* is used 1688 times in the Old Testament and 478 times in the New Testament, for a total of 2166 times. This does not include the implied version of *now*. Each time that a commandment was issued, it was made with the understanding that it would be valid and effective in the *moment* of declaration.

The number of times a word is used in the Bible is strongly correlated to its significance. Based on this standard given to Biblical writing, the conclusion is that the word *now* is far more significant than even the word *day*. The word *now* in today's understanding is what is referred to as being present or in the moment. Full attention in the moment of an activity is the highest expression of love in a relationship and the most effective use of time.

The current words related to *time* in our American culture are often related to speed. An example would be how quickly a project could be accomplished. Words such as *fast, slow* or *haste* and *sluggish* are words related to things that can be done over a unit of time. The word *soon* in prophecy is interesting when compared to today's frame of reference. Revelation 22:7 reports Jesus as saying, "And behold, I am coming soon. Blessed is the one who keeps the words of the prophecy of this book." His idea of *soon* has extended for almost two thousand years.

In contrast, the Biblical context of the word *fast* was used to mean holding tightly or in reference to dietary restrictions when special times of reverence were declared. Fasting was practiced to limit self-indulgence. My contention is that holding fast to God, as a priority even over food, is symbolic of one's dedication to time with Him. Jesus says in John 4:34, "My food is to do the will of Him who sent me and to accomplish His work." This declaration implies to me that it was more important for Jesus to hold *fast* to His Father, God's will than to feed Himself with food. Can you think of a situation where enjoying the presence of God or doing a project lead by God is more important to you than eating?

The word *faster* was used in reference to the heart rate when one might get nervous or anxious. *Faster* was also used to compare the rate of running between one person and another. The word *present* was used only in reference to a gift.

Biblically, distance was also referenced in terms of time. The most frequent use of time to represent distance was the number of days' journey by foot to a location. This was based on approximately 20 miles traversed per day. One example is reported in Genesis 30:36 where it describes how Laban distanced himself from Jacob and his flock of goats by a distance of a three days' journey.

On my trip across to Acadia National Park, distance questions were being answered in terms of time required to get to a specific location. Today, with traffic jams, road construction and perhaps natural disasters, travel by car is frequently related to many factors other than simply distance. Could this current development in the perception of distance be directing you to more Biblical thinking? Could God be seeking to get your attention in this way?

Biblical Standard Time

The following authors give descriptions of God's time in the Old Testament. David in Psalms 84:10 said, "For a day in your courts is better than a thousand outside." God's intention for His time is given in Isaiah 49:8 as, "In a favorable time, I have answered you." Solomon in his wisdom describes God's timing as, "There is an appointed time for everything. And there is a time for every event under heaven—A *time* to give birth and a *time* to die; A *time* to plant and a *time* to uproot what is planted. A *time* to kill and a *time* to heal; A *time* to tear down and a *time* to build up..." (Ecclesiastes 3:1–8). The Byrds, a vocal group of the 1960s, used many of these verses in their popular song titled "Turn! Turn! Turn!"

A year of time in Biblical writings was filled with customs, feasts and celebrations. See Exodus 23:14, and 2Chronicles 8:13. Modern calendars and timepieces were not available. Today the year is understood to be one rotation of the earth around the sun, however, thousands of years ago, the earth was deemed the center of heavenly orbits. It was not until the 16th and 17th centuries that Galileo began changing the perspective on celestial movements. The Italian observational astronomer brought forward the idea of heliocentrism, where the sun is the center of our solar system, over geocentrism, the earth being the center around which the sun rotates. This concept was introduced just a few hundred years after people finally accepted that the earth was round.

Biblical references to a year of time was used in much the same way that we refer to years as with age, periods of time that a ruler reigned or events lasted. Frequently, the event would be referred to as having occurred in the numerical year during the reign of a specific priest or king as in the Book of Esther. In Esther 2:16 it says, "So Esther was taken to King Ahasuerus to his royal palace in the tenth month which is the month Tebeth, in the seventh *year* of his reign." Since calendars were not available for use as they are today, the frame of reference was during the reign of King Ahasuerus, several thousand years ago. Today, the Japanese still implement this frame of reference as in 2006, they referred to that year as the 18th year of Emperor Akihito's reign.

The division of years into months and days was primarily set up in the fourth day of creation from Genesis 1:13–19. The year, as we know it today, is 365 days, 5 hours, 48 minutes and 46 seconds. Every four years we get an extra day to shore up the extra time beyond the 365 days of the other three years. We call this a leap year and it occurs as February 29th every four years. This book was started on February 29 of 2016, as there was an extra day of *time* to collect my thoughts and write.

Each year is almost exactly represented by thirteen lunar months of close to 28 days each. The use of the month or "moon" time is closely related to a woman's ovulation and menses period. Physiologically, this monthly time period is also associated with vital hormonal cycles that lead to fertility and mood changes. It is no small coincidence that the most romantic visual moon will often correlate with the most likely time of a successful conception. The next question might be, when *is* the most romantic picture of the graphic and inspirational moon?

Each lunar month is represented as the time required for the visual moon to go through its four main phases. These phases begin with the new moon, the completely invisible moon, due to a lack of reflection from the sun. The new noon designated the beginning of a new month and was to be heralded in by trumpets for several days. It was also a significant time of worship. See Numbers 10:10 and Ezekiel 46:3. The first quarter, which looks like a half moon lit up in the sky, has its curvature on the right as it is growing to a full moon. From the bright shining full moon, it begins to diminish to the third quarter, and the predominant curvature of the moon is seen on the left. To summarize, the moon expands with its curvature on the right and shrinks to nothing visible when the curvature is on the left. The next time you see the moon, check for its curvature and determine if it is growing to a full moon or shrinking to a new one.

The moon and its phases had economic significance in relation to sea travel, fishing and recreation. It was noted for thousands of years that the tides were at their highest when the moon was either full or at the time of a new moon, having no visibility in the sky. This was especially true in spring.

The new moon is clearly the beginning of a new month. When the moon is full, several nights depict its fullness and thus it is more difficult to determine the peak of its cycle. The new moon was considered a sign for new beginnings, and an important time of worship, as beginning the day in worship is important, Numbers 10:10 and Isaiah 66:23.

The gravitational impact of the moon on the surface of the ocean also has its impact on breaking the water of childbirth. For years, I worked in a modest community hospital known as a birthing center for mothers in northern California. The rumor was that far more new births occurred when there was a full moon. This report was considered to be a superstition, at best, however, the nurses in the obstetric ward informed me that they would always double up on supplies as the full moon was approaching anyway.

The time involved for each of the four major phases of the moon are an approximate representation of the seven-day week we use today. These seven days date back thousands of years to the first days of creation. Moses initially reported the first seven days in Genesis 1:1 to Genesis 2:4. The first chapter of Genesis presents what was created on each of the first six days; the first day was the day of light; the second day was the day of heaven; the third day was the day of land, sea and vegetation; the fourth day was the day of sun, moon and stars; the fifth day was the day of fish and fowl; and the sixth day was the day of man. In this chapter, there has been some debate as to how long these days of creation actually were since such remarkable events occurred on each day. Moses used the words, "And there was evening and there was morning," to define the time for each day. See Genesis 1:1–31.

The seventh day is described in Genesis chapter two as the day that God rested from all of His work. God sanctified that day in Exodus 20:8–11 and it became the Jewish custom of worship. The term Sabbath is the root word of sabbatical rest and is used as a break from routine activities. Rest is valuable in restoring your physiology and allows greater efficiency during the time allotted for work and other activities. In God's provision, the time of rest on the Sabbath allows Him to restore your spiritual wellbeing also. The complete discussion and value of this Sabbath rest according to God's plan of sanctification is beyond the scope of this book. It is discussed more completely in other publications and will be covered in a review of the third day of creation in my forthcoming book.

Observing the Sabbath in eternity is mentioned in Isaiah 66:22–23, "'For just as the new heavens and the new earth which I make will endure before Me,' declares the LORD, 'So your offspring and your name will endure. And it shall be from new moon to new moon and from Sabbath to Sabbath, All mankind will come to bow down before Me,' says the LORD." These verses emphasize the practice of timely and periodic worship based on the monthly and weekly cycles of time. Resting in the wisdom of God's word cannot be underestimated. As it states in Psalm 119:27, "Make me understand the way of Your precepts, so I will meditate on Your wonders."

The seven-day week closely matches the time for each of the four phases of the moon. This was used in Biblical times for travel or tasks that took longer than a day but less than a month. As may be seen from the chart on page 42, months and weeks were far less frequently referred to when compared to *days, years* and *time* in general.

Referring to *until* a specified time, or to explicitly *wait* was given far more significance than the *future*, *lifetime* or even *eternity*. These terms reflect the significance of how time was being spent based on how frequently these words were used in the Bible. Of note is that events occurring beyond the *now* time frame are far less clear, predictable or even worth considering. What is important is how time is being spent until these future events happen. Specifically, something that *is* "eternal" presents itself with greater significance than eternity because what *is* eternal, is so in the present, the *now*.

The word *period* versus *season* had distinctions regarding time. *Period* used in the Bible generally referred to times extending from one week to forty years. *Season* was used for allocations of time less than a year often in relation to weather, crops or animal patterns, Jeremiah 8:7. *Season* often related to breeding and birthing. It was minimally used to refer to that which enhances the flavor of food or speech. Both the words *period* and *season* had subjective parameters as opposed to definitive characteristics such as sunrise to sunset for the word *day*, the new moon of *month or* the pattern of the sun for each *year*.

Biblical Prophetic Time

Speaking of the word *day*, Ezekiel 4:6 defines the value of a prophetic day as being one year. The prophetic day, as a time frame, is extensively written of in the book of Daniel and Revelation. An example of one day being one prophetic year is the test of faith written of in Revelation 2:10. The author John quotes Jesus as saying that tribulation will befall some who are thrown into prison for 10 days. It is believed that these 10 days referred to the prophecy of imprisonment that occurred over a ten-year period from 303 to 313 A.D. and was terminated when Constantine became emperor.

The prophetic day to year concept is introduced in Numbers 14:34 where God states, "According to the number of the days in which you spied out the land, forty days, for each day you shall bear your guilt one year, namely forty years, and you shall know My rejection."

The word *time* is also used extensively in the Bible, both for its conventional meaning and in prophetic verses. Revelation 12:14 portrays the word *time* to indicate a prophetic period equivalent to a year. "But the two wings of the great eagle were given to the woman, so that she could fly into the wilderness to her place, where she was nourished for a *time* and *times* and half a *time*, from the presence of the serpent." Biblical writings have used the "time and times and half a time" to designate three and one-half years or 1260 days. Those 1260 days are then a representation of 1260 years, which later became known in history as the years of papal supremacy. This period is believed to have been from 538 to 1798 A.D. of papal rule.

Confirming this time period, Revelation 11:2 refers to 42 months, also considered three and one-half years or 1260 days. These prophetic days are viewed as prophetic years and represent the same time period of from 538 to 1798 A.D. Jesus cited that "Jerusalem will be trampled underfoot by the Gentiles, until the times (years) of the Gentiles be fulfilled" in Luke 21:24.

The word period is also used prophetically to denote a year of time when preceded by a number as in Daniel 4:16. Daniel writes "And let seven periods of time pass over him." Here he is referring to a seven year period of time during which King Nebuchadnezzar was left in the wild, and after which he recognized the sovereignty of God.

Measuring Daily Biblical Time

Lastly, the word *hour* is only used in the New Testament and primarily refers to an increment of time less than a day. Measuring the time of an hour in the earliest years of human history might have included variations of a clepsydra, water clock or a clepsammia, sand clock. The hour glass as we know it today was not customarily used until at least 335 A.D., although the earliest versions were attributed to use in Alexandria, Egypt, in 150 B.C. The hourglass consistency varies with quality of the sand, its coarseness, bulb size and neck width. The hourglass may be used indefinitely by inverting the bulbs once the upper bulb is empty, however, this requires consistent rotation manually every hour.

The *hour* of Biblical times was most likely sourced from the sundial, which also originated many thousands of years ago. What must be kept in mind is the diverse nature of the shadow of the sun from area to area and the mechanics of each sundial unit such that the uniformity of an hour was highly unlikely. For a given referenced area, the sundial was useful in measuring work times, daily activities and had marginal if any use after sunset.

Reference to the word *will* is also timely. The word *will* has a future connotation, or even a prophetic one. The seed of *will* begins in the now. As such, the word *will* is listed 5,788 times in the Bible, 4,545 times in the Old Testament and 1,243 times in the New Testament. The concept of *will* in the Bible refers to the *will* of God, the *will* of intention, the consequences of what might result from an action and most importantly that God *will* provide a source of salvation. Many of the Old Testament verses refer to this coming of Jesus as in Isaiah 9:6, which reads:

> For a child *will* be born to us, a son *will* be
> given to us; And the government *will* rest on His

shoulders; And His name *will* be called Wonderful Counselor, Mighty God, Eternal Father, Prince of Peace.

The list of words and the frequency of their use for time below correlate to their significance. The increment of time that is consistently the same is *now* or what could be considered as being the "present." The word *will* is rooted in the *now* as given above.

Which Day Is Which?

Jesus worshiped on the Sabbath, Luke 4:16. Why has Sunday been chosen for worship instead of on the Sabbath? In Revelation 1:10, the apostle John reports:

> *I was in the Spirit on the Lord's day,*
> *and I heard behind me a loud voice*
> *like the sound of a trumpet,*

Revelation was written well after the death and resurrection of Jesus. In Mark 2:27–28,

> *Jesus said to them, "The Sabbath was made for man,*
> *and not man for the Sabbath. So the Son of Man is*
> *Lord even of the Sabbath."*

Since man was created on the sixth day, Genesis 1:26, this makes sense. Man was created before God recommended implementing the rest referred to in the fourth commandment of Exodus 20. The Sabbath rest was declared as the day of rest, holiness and blessings for mankind in Exodus 20:8–11. God blessed the Sabbath day and made it holy, thus the Lord's Day is the Sabbath if these three scriptures are considered together.

Looking at the progression of Creation, the first day, Sunday, was the day of light. Man was created on the sixth day and then the seventh day became available for rest. Why would one want to rest on the first day before they were created on the sixth day?

The Sabbath day, or the seventh day, is the day that God specifically works in us, if we let Him, to transform us into the divine nature of Christ. Ezekiel 20:12 describes this day as God's declaration to us.

> *Also, I gave them My Sabbaths to be a sign between*
> *Me and them, that they might know that I am the*
> *Lord who sanctifies them.*

This promise of sanctification was designed to last for future generations as written in Exodus 31:13:

> *But as for you, speak to the sons of Israel, saying,*
> *'You shall surely observe My Sabbaths; for this*
> *is a sign between Me and you throughout your*
> *generations, that you my know that I am*
> *the Lord who sanctifies you.'*

In this day and age of business, who could not benefit from a little more rest? To have God working in you is an added bonus. God claims the Sabbath to be holy to you. One of the ways of looking at holiness, according to my godmother, Joy, is that it is your "wholeness." Who would not enjoy *being* and feeling more "whole" or complete as an individual?

This is the sanctification process described in 2Peter 1:3–4:

> *Seeing that His divine power has granted to us*
> *everything pertaining to life and godliness, through*
> *the true knowledge of Him who called us by His own*
> *glory and excellence. For by these He has granted to*

us His precious and magnificent promises,
so that by them you may become partakers of the
divine nature, having escaped the corruption that is
in the world by lust.

Philippians 1:6 echoes this promise, stating:

For I am confident of this very thing, that He who
began a good work in you will perfect it until the day
of Christ Jesus.

It is God's own work of sanctification that transforms us in the likeness of Christ and it is specifically implemented on His holy day, the Sabbath, as you come to Him and rest.

Thus the apostle Paul reminds us in Hebrews 4:11 that:

Therefore let us be diligent to enter that rest, so that
no one will fall, through following the same example
of disobedience.

According to Psalm 118:24, "This is the day which the *Lord* has made; let us rejoice and be glad in it." Every day is a day to celebrate in His presence; however, it is the Sabbath that is specifically set aside for the sanctification process by God Himself. It is a day that stands apart from the other six days of work. Genesis 2:2–3 cites how God rested on the seventh day, blessed it and sanctified it. This day offers distinct benefits of holiness from God's own work in us. It is His command from Exodus 20:8–11. Sunday worship is not a Biblical practice. Sabbath worship is.

Relative Biblical Time

The New Testament relates perspectives on time by Paul in Galatians 4:4. It states, "When the fullness of time came, God sent forth His Son, born of a woman, born under the Law." And in

2Timothy 3:1 Paul writes, "In the last days, difficult times will come." Peter continues on this theme with, "In the last days mockers will come following after their own lusts," as is written in 2Peter 3:3. Also, 2Peter 3:8 says, "But do not let this one fact escape your notice, beloved, that with the Lord, one day is like a thousand years, and a thousand years like one day."

Another aspect of time is time during sleep. During sleep there is no recollection of the passage of time. How many times have you rolled over in the early morning, for "just another ten minutes" to discover that an hour and a half had passed?

In Christ, those who "sleep," in other words die, have no recollection of the passage of time either. They are the ones that 1Thessalonians 4:15 refers to as the ones who rise first. "According to the Lord's word, we tell you that we who are still alive, who are left until the coming of the Lord, will certainly not precede those who have fallen asleep." Upon awakening on this last day, their first awareness will be the face of Jesus, with no understanding of how much time has passed since their death. See chapter five, Living in God's Timing, page 83.

What lends credibility to the Bible is seen in prophecy, as things predicted come to pass. An example would be the prediction of a Messiah, how and why He would come as well as His certainty and impact. There are over 300 verses in the Old Testament pointing to these aspects of His coming and they came to pass. The Old Testament covers a time span of over four thousand years.

In contrast, the New Testament has over five times as many verses referring to the second coming of Christ. Expansion of this prophecy is beyond the scope of this writing and is addressed in other publications. The New Testament was written over a much shorter period of only a hundred years or so. We are now past the two thousand year mark, which began at the time of Christ's birth. Some of the predicted events have already been established. In each instance, the missing factor regarding Christ's birth or second coming was or is *when* He would be born or enter at His second coming, His first or second Advent. God only knew or knows of each of these two events for certain. In the meantime, His recommendations for our preparation is clear and begins with what must be done *now*.

The words in the Bible were written over a time span of 1600 years by 40 authors and include 66 different books. A tapestry of events, symbolism, prophecy and maxims unites the common thread of verses in these books such that it would appear as though there is only ONE author. In history, the events of the Bible have come to pass as predicted and the promises of God are reliable. Biblicists agree that God's Word, as written in the Bible, is the true wisdom from God Himself, who deals without a clock, yet with precision.

BIBLICAL WORDS USED TO REFERENCE TIME

WORD	(times)	OLD TESTAMENT	NEW TESTAMENT
Now	(2166)	1688	478
Day	(2047)	1654	393
Year	(750)	678	72
Time	(726)	504	222
Until	(549)	422	127
Day of the Lord	(460)*	437	23
Forever	(323)	272	51
Night	(315)	252	63
Month	(237)	217	20
Wait	(142)	113	29
Today	(190)	161	29
Immediately	(106)	5	101
Next	(103)	70	33
Hour	(85)		85
Eternal	(75)	70	5
Soon	(74)	58	16
Moment	(28)	19	9
Season	(27)	19	8
Week	(26)	17	9
Future	(22)	19	3
Day of Judgment	(17)*	8	9
Lifetime	(10)	5	5
Instant	(8)	8	
Eternity	(7)	5	2
Will	(5788)	4545	1243

*Day of the Lord and Day of Judgment are included in the 2047 total for the word Day.

Chapter Three

God's Direction for Your Time

God's direction has a purpose
That is set up by design.
He knows you want fulfillment
And rewards those so inclined.

We all travel around the sun at the same rate.

The fourth day from Genesis chapter one reminds us of the precision of God's timing. This was the day the Sun, Moon and Stars were created. Our common measure of time, the 24-hour day, began with this fourth day. Each of the days reported in Genesis chapter one recount "there was evening and there was morning, the _____ day." This framework for time was set up in preparation for His creation of mankind on the sixth day.

You were created for a purpose unique to you and for your contribution in service with your time on earth.

How God Designed You to Spend Your Time

Contrary to some commentaries, God created you in His own image. He loves you so much that he wants nothing more than to keep you in relationship with Him. Not by robotic design but by your choice. He has given you the promises, provisions, priorities and His presence if and when you choose to take Him up on His offer. This is powerful.

The omniscient, omnipotent and omnipresent ONE wants to be with you! You and God are a decided majority. He wants to be your sufficiency, your abundance and your JOY in life.

Thou wilt make known to me the path of life; in thy presence is fullness of joy; in thy right hand there are treasures forever. (Psalms 16:11)

I love those who love me; and those who diligently seek me will find me. Riches and honor are with me, enduring wealth and righteousness. My fruit is better than gold, even pure gold, and my yield than choicest silver. I walk in the way of righteousness, in the midst of the paths of justice, to endow those who love me with wealth, that I may fill their lives with treasures. (Proverbs 8:17–21)

Time alone with God must be your highest priority and deepest joy, even if it is only for a moment at a time. As in marriage, your true love is the light of your life on earth. In this way, God wants that relationship with you in the spiritual connection of comfort, security, love and true joyful creativity. Through Jesus He, the bridegroom provides all that you need. You individually or collectively, male or female, are intended to be His Divine Bride. This is true whether you are single or not. As Isaiah 62:5 says, "And as the bridegroom rejoices over the bride, so your God will rejoice over you."

If you look carefully at God's plan for creation in Genesis chapter one, His love for you provided the rationale for the most productive use of your time. The talents given to you by God are to be used to "be fruitful and multiply."

The Four "Geniacle" Commandments

With this background in mind, I would like to review the *four* commandments that were first given by God to His first creation of man. As the heading above indicates, I call them the "Geniacle" commandments because they are the first four things that God told man to do in the Book of Genesis. Very early on in Genesis 1:28, God said, "Be fruitful and multiply, and fill the earth, and subdue it; and rule over the fish of the sea and over the birds of the sky, and over every living thing that moves on the earth." To be fruitful and to multiply are activities that allow you to fully express your divine nature, and lift you up to the level of significance that you were meant to live. This is a fulfilling life.

Being fruitful comes in many shapes and sizes, from procreation to landscaping, cooking, photography and more. Over the years mankind has created, invented and developed so many useful things, all of which have brought humanity the conveniences available to you today. Our current global population attests to the ability of mankind to multiply successfully. God has also created man with the ability to serve one other with individual and unique gifts. Thus, living in community allows for the balance of give and take. Implementing this form of contribution builds individual significance and fulfillment. This is an important form of creating your JOY.

> *Commit your works to the Lord and your plans will*
> *be established. (Proverbs 16:3)*

With this one verse of Genesis 1:28 given above, two important commandments are presented; be fruitful and multiply, number one. This command is to implement your contribution to others with your unique gifts. The second directive is to rule over the earth, over all living things, and subdue it. You were meant to be a steward of the earth and its resources.

The third commandment is seen in Genesis 2:16–17. "And the Lord God commanded the man saying, 'From any tree of the garden you may eat freely; but from the tree of the knowledge of good and evil you shall not eat, for in the day that you eat from it you shall surely die.'"

This special direction is significant because the knowledge of good and evil could be considered as the starting point of judgment. Judgment or labeling is one of the most heartbreaking limitations that man imposes on his thinking and thus imparts an obligation of *time* that is not fruitful. How much time do you spend judging?

This time of deliberation may take hours over days and takes away from the time needed to live in the solution, the creation of your new future. Living in the anger or resentment of judgment also sets you up for mistakes in the future, distractions and the bondage of time.

Do you feel judged? Valuable time may be lost worrying about what others may think of you or what you have done. This is the beauty of knowing and doing the God-given desire you were meant to implement.

Judgment is the groundwork for comparing, complaining, gossiping, anger, resentment, blame, ingratitude, lack of forgiveness, animosity, fear, guilt, depression and worry. These are the self-imposed thoughts that create blocks to God's flow of love. In today's daily activities, they give rise to stress and stagnation. Stress destroys health by compromising sleep and impairs loving relationship. Stress or pain may give attention to learning that a solution is needed to that problem brought on by stress. As has been attributed to Plato, "Necessity is the mother of invention." However, that solution will most likely evolve from a place of peace.

Feelings of gratitude, passionate excitement, happiness, inspiration, hope, contentment, love, joy and peace are what allow you to be creative. They are also the source of your health and wellness. From the place of love and joy there is a calm state of being that simply allows new ideas to be considered and performance enhanced.

You have the capability of thinking only one thought at a time. Once a pattern of negative deliberation takes hold, it not only consumes mental and emotional time, but it crowds out positive thoughts and creative solutions to what you must do. Training your thoughts is a valuable spiritual discipline.

An example of the above concept occurred several years ago in my life. I was in graduate school and remodeling my home. My job in sales required lots of travel. I was dealing with some family issues and not in the best of health. One afternoon, while at home, I had a list of "to-dos" on my agenda. I was beginning to get nervous about what to do first. Would I have enough time? Would I have to do things over again because they did not work in the first place? I began to get concerned over the consequences of not getting things done that I thought needed to be taken care of. Then out of the clear blue and perhaps out of a sheer need to "escape," I began reading the Bible.

What I discovered while reading was that most of what I was concerned about really did not matter. I surrendered to the outcome. Somehow I was lead to simply let go and implement my version of GPS, *God's Perfect Solution.*

It was a release that allowed me to *be* in the energy of the moment, without feeling overwhelmed. Once I stopped reading, I got up and did the most important things that needed to be done with a flow of energy that felt effortless. It was almost like an "out of this world" experience with no resentment, no aggravation, and no worry.

Human Being to Human Doing

If you look further into the story of Adam and Eve that is given in Genesis 3:7, the eating of the fruit resulted in a new awareness of their nakedness. They then sewed fig leaves together and made themselves loin coverings. They noticed their nakedness, considered themselves to be living in a condition of insufficiency (judgment, guilt) and then *chose* to reposition themselves from living as human *beings* to human *doings*.

How have your feelings of inadequacy held you back from your true self-expression?

Many times what is done reflects a need to "look good" instead of just being who you are. Living from a need to "look good," "save face" and stand beyond judgment is an unrealistic expectation for yourself. It wastes time because pleasing others is bound to result in dissatisfactions. Other people already come from a place of imperfection and bring their own weaknesses into such judgment. God loves you anyway, no matter what.

Back to Adam and Eve, they did not want to consider God's provision as enough. In a way, they *could* not because they broke the trusting relationship with Him by being disobedient. They determined that His perfect plan needed to be supplemented by their *doings*. Up until this experience of eating the forbidden fruit, often called "the fall," Adam and Eve were living in the bliss of complete provision by their source of contentment, God.

Recognizing that they had sinned, they began the pattern of covering up for their actions. They hid themselves from the presence of God. They pre-judged God's response when He would have been willing to accept their confession and determination to get back on the track of obedience. The time used for sewing the loin coverings and then hiding was *done* in an effort to overcome their brief act of disobedience. Overcoming disobedience with *time* and effort has not improved in efficiency for over six thousand years.

When God questioned their behavior, they implemented other time-robbing practices. They began the cycle of blame and rationalizations. Eve blamed the serpent for telling her that eating of the fruit would not result in death. Adam blamed Eve for having given the fruit to him, and that, after all, God gave him Eve as a wife. This was how Adam tried to blame God for his act of disobedience.

Being defensive in this way is characteristic of human behavior, however, how much time is spent coming up with these types of excuses? Describing the rational is really not the issue. What needs to be recognized, is the truth of what happened. They were told not to eat, and they ate. That is that. Here is an example.

Recently, I was asked to participate in a program that my friend really wanted me to engage in. She asked, and I politely said "No." There was a long silence. I could tell that she was disappointed, however, the answer was still "No." She continued to probe and spend the time she felt necessary to change my mind, however, the answer was still "No." The fact that I said "No" had nothing to do with how much I valued her as a friend, or that I had any preferences regarding how she chose to spend her time. Bantering back and forth is simply not a good use of time.

How much time do you spend blaming and rationalizing your behaviors or even the behaviors of others? How does all of that defensive time create your best life *now*?

Another example of the human *doings* that result from feelings of judgment is the story of Cain and Abel. Cain felt angry when he compared his sacrifice to the sacrifice given by his brother Abel. God noticed that his countenance had fallen. In Genesis 4:7, God says, "If you do well, will not your countenance be lifted up? And if you do not do well, sin is crouching at the door; and its desire is for you, but *you must master it.*"

Thus the fourth commandment given in Genesis is *to master sin.* Cain acted out of frustration because his offering did not look good when compared to the offering of Abel. His sin of destruction, the murder of his brother Abel, emerged out of his comparing and his pride. Cain was not able to see himself of value in the eyes of God as a human *being.* He equated his value by his *doings,* the provision of an inappropriate sacrifice.

Out of desperation, Cain had to eliminate what he thought was the source of his disappointment, his brother. His solution was an act of *doing,* taking matters into his own hands, instead of seeking a higher level of *being.* That higher level of *being* consists of confessing that his sacrifice was incorrect, seeking forgiveness, and changing his approach for future offerings. Beginning anew, as the New Testament refers to in Philippians, is what God has designed for His Beloved creation, you. As the apostle Paul has written,

> *Brethren, I do not regard myself as having laid hold*
> *of it yet; but one thing I do: forgetting what lies*
> *behind and reaching forward to what lies ahead,*
> *I press on... toward the goal for the prize of the*
> *upward call of God in Christ Jesus.*
> *(Philippians 3:13–14)*

What is more important is that comparing leads to despairing. God wants you to gain your worth from His love for you as

His beloved human *being* not in your *doings*. It is your love of and for God that then compels you to *do* loving, kind and glorifying things. That is His will for you.

> *Therefore be careful how you walk, not as unwise*
> *men, but as wise, making the most of your time,*
> *because the days are evil. So then do not be foolish,*
> *but understand what the will of the Lord is.*
> *(Ephesians 5:15–17)*

You Get to Choose

Noticing evaluations of inadequacy in your behavior can lead to a host of negative feelings that get imbedded in your thoughts. Stopping this pattern of self-judgment requires a disciplined approach. There needs to be a way of recognizing the undesirable behavior, deciding how you would like to handle it in the future and then moving on. The past needs to stay in the past. *Now* is the time to plan on how you want to create your new future by choosing a different thought.

As stated earlier, God's first command in Genesis is "*be fruitful and multiply.*" Launching a new creative activity that spurs you on can be an effective remedy to the negative feelings and thoughts brought on by judgment. A loving community or a supportive partner in these circumstances is helpful also. Those who have developed a strong relationship and faith in God may run to Him first for confession and repentance in prayer. At this point, wisdom comes in remembering:

> *Seek first His Kingdom and His righteousness;*
> *and all these things shall be added to you.*
> *(Matthew 6:33)*

In the above instance of self-evaluation, it may be helpful to focus on the perfection of God. Can you accept that you are simply not completely perfect yet? If you need perfection, focus on the divine perfection of your Creator. This is an example of how Matthew 6:33 may be used. You are on a divine journey of perfection in Christ that may be called sanctification.

Also of note is that overcoming sin begins with a choice of focus. As you focus on God, you can enjoy the truth of 1Corinthians 1:30. Here the apostle Paul reminds us that God is at work to see that those who are in Christ Jesus benefit from the wisdom of God, His righteousness, sanctification and redemption. It is not your effort, that none should boast, it is God's work in you as you change your focus.

Along with this recommendation is 1Timothy 6:12, where Paul reminds us that the battle is not in the doing but the *abiding* (time connected to the source). It is your fight to stay in your faith with God. It is your faith in God that will allow that transformation to occur in you, as you hold on to His promises. "Fight the good fight of faith; take hold of the eternal life to which you were called, and you made the good confession in the presence of many witnesses."

The chart on page 54 is a graphic representation of what Matthew 6:33 means to me.

The enjoyment of your life is a function of time and efforts or energy spent to get what you want. The letters **J O Y** represent **J** for Jesus and the time focused on relationship with Him in Bible study and prayer; **O** represents time focused on other people and things that enhance your life. These other people and things represent relationships, career, material things and entertainment. **Y** is for "you" at the intersection of the time, (vertical) and the effort/ energy (horizontal) lines.

When you are focused on the "O" of your life, you may find it difficult to spend enough time developing that relationship with Jesus. The top chart shows how much less time is spent with Him as compared to the amount of time and effort used in getting what you want in your life of *doing*.

The bottom chart shows what happens when greater amounts of time are spent in relationship with Jesus. The line that represents the energy of *doing* on your part (horizontal) is dramatically reduced. The same benefit of daily needs and relationship with others are achieved, but with much less effort/energy.

This reminds me of how God fights your battles, "No weapon that is formed against you shall prosper…" (Isaiah 54:17); how God provides for your needs, "Be anxious for nothing, but in everything by prayer and supplication with thanksgiving let your requests be made known to God…" (Philippians 4:6); and how God sanctifies you, "He who began a good work in you will perfect it until the day of Christ Jesus" (Philippians 1:6).

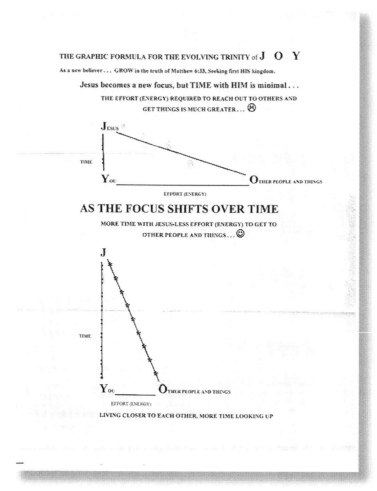

THE GRAPHIC FORMULA FOR THE EVOLVING TRINITY of **J O Y**

As a new believer ... GROW in the truth of Matthew 6:33, Seeking first HIS kingdom.

Jesus becomes a new focus, but TIME with HIM is minimal ...

THE EFFORT (ENERGY) REQUIRED TO REACH OUT TO OTHERS AND
GET THINGS IS MUCH GREATER ... ☹

AS THE FOCUS SHIFTS OVER TIME

MORE TIME WITH JESUS-LESS EFFORT (ENERGY) TO GET TO
OTHER PEOPLE AND THINGS ... ☺

LIVING CLOSER TO EACH OTHER, MORE TIME LOOKING UP

I love the way that God sanctifies you in your growing relationship with Jesus. He does the work over time as you abide in Him. Instead of living as a human *doing*, it is so much more energy efficient to let God bring things together, than for you to agonize over the details. Your transformation simply flows out of *being* in a relationship with your forever friend, Jesus.

Your life is the crowning glory of your *time* on earth. The best part is you get to choose the jewels that go onto that crown. God gave you a free "will" for that purpose and you get to choose how to use it. Ideally, you would make the choices that give you your best life *now*. Taking responsibility for your choices *now* is paramount.

Now is the operative word because although you have lived a number of years, what exists at this very moment is all you know for sure. You can decide through your thoughts and the vision of your dreams what you want, right *now*. Do you want more love? Better communication? Do you want a new job or career? Are you committed to a different way of *being?* Change your focus.

Focus on God and He will either take you there or change your dream of desire. You put into motion what you want by making the decision. Adding passion to that decision propels the process even faster. Changing your thoughts, deciding with courage and conviction, is the first step to the "you" you want to be. You must completely visualize in detail what your best life looks like right *now*, knowing and believing in faith that God will put in motion His GPS, *God's Perfect Solution*. That desire for you was given to you by God, and He will see that you bring it about, through Him.

Delight in the Lord and He will give you the desires
of your heart. (Psalm 37:4)

Here is an example. As a younger person, I always wanted to live in Santa Cruz. My family was living in San Jose over the hill, some 30 miles away. Santa Cruz was a resort community with difficult access over winding roads; few job opportunities and higher priced living. It was also too far from my family life for me to move there. I had three sisters and two brothers all younger and living at home at the time. Going to the beach in Santa Cruz was one of my favorite things to do, however, it was just too far for me to get to all of the time.

I became a pharmacist and several of my co-workers in San Jose lived in Santa Cruz. I was intimidated by the daily commute over the curvy mountain road that brought people "over the hill," but I still dreamed of living there someday. I had moved out and was on my own, but I did not feel at peace making such a dramatic move and tackling the daily commute.

Then I got a job in sales. That was a bit scary at first because it had a lot of travel and learning. Part of my territory of business was in Santa Cruz. Perhaps God was giving me this opportunity to move to my dream city. With this job, He was definitely training me to cope with traveling over 250 miles daily or even staying the night out of town. At that point, my territory was from Fresno and Visalia up to Stockton and Lodi, over to Walnut Creek, South San Francisco and down to Monterey.

Since I had to fly to other parts of the country quite a bit, I moved to San Carlos, which was only 18 miles from the San Francisco Airport. Pharmaceutical selling was a completely different game than working in a drug store. I was challenged by the new career focus and travel, but this also strengthened my relationship and trust in God. He was teaching me to be more confident with new and unusual assignments, people and places.

Over several years, my territory shrank to covering only San Jose to Monterey. I was living 25 miles out of my territory by then, so I thought it might be a good idea to move to a more central location. At that point, it was either Santa Cruz or San Juan Bautista. Unfortunately, Santa Cruz had higher priced homes and I could not afford to move there, so I picked the latter. Home prices in San Juan Bautista were climbing modestly, but I had a realtor who managed the purchase of a home for me at a great price.

During these years of sales work, I had gotten very involved with ministry, Bible studies and writing songs based on scripture. Through my interest in health and learning God's Word, I met a minister who also sang and wrote music. We decided to get married and build a Bible-based fellowship.

Once married, my husband said we could live anywhere in support of my sales activities. After two and a half years, the home in San Juan Bautista had more than doubled in price. Finally, we were able to buy a home in a new development of Santa Cruz.

Now my biggest joy is living close enough to everything I need so that I can walk. Thus, I rarely get stuck in traffic or have difficulties finding a place to park. This dream of mine came together in God's timing and on God's path. He even thought of things that I enjoy, but forgot to put on my wish list. He fulfilled the desires of my heart, as I focused on Him. As is given in Ephesians 3:20, "Now to Him who is able to do exceeding abundantly beyond all that we ask or think, according to the power that works within us…"

God Gave You That Desire

This is a powerful concept because desire, at its root, means "of the Father." *De* meaning "from" and *sire* meaning "Father." You were made with burning dreams and desires in your heart. These are the dreams that get you out of bed in the morning. These are the dreams that motivate you and give you the energy to move forward.

On a generic level, you want to achieve that beacon of significance. You want to leave the world a better place and you want your legacy to count for good. How do you know what God's purpose for you is? It rests with your passion to serve, to connect and to express those God given talents that God put in His treasure, YOU. This is the value of knowing you can have faith in the purpose that God put you here for.

That faith is what keeps you going regardless of the circumstances. You will have opposition. You will have obstacles to overcome and you will strengthen your resolve and character in the process. Consider all of those times when people said it could not be done. The world is flat! Flying is for the birds! Who could possibly use a horseless carriage on these rocky roads? Computers are not practical. Those objections did not stop the dream process. God will always stand beside you to the fulfillment of your dream because they came from Him to begin with.

Looking at what is available or conventional today does not mean it has to stay that way. What you move towards, through your intentions, will provide the next step and then the next step, when you step out in faith. That dream and that desire are there for a purpose. You must simply have the faith to hold onto that vision of yours.

> *I can do all things through Him who strengthens me.*
> *(Philippians 4:13)*

God blesses your efforts in living your desires because it fulfills the purpose that He created you to live out, *to be fruitful.* You must be bold in your purposeful time on earth. You must fulfill your God-given legacy and let your light shine.

> *Let your light shine before men in such a way that*
> *they may see your good works, and glorify your*
> *Father who is in heaven. (Matthew 5:16)*

> *They looked to Him and were radiant, and their*
> *faces shall never be ashamed. (Psalm 34:5)*

Those who have insight will shine brightly like the
brightness of the expanse of the heavens, and those
who bring the many to righteousness like the stars
forever and ever. (Daniel 12:3)

His master said to him, "Well done, good and
faithful servant. You were faithful with a few things;
I will put you in charge of many things, enter into
the joy of your master." (Matthew 25:21)

Christ's Object Lessons *by Ellen White states, "Our*
time belongs to God. Every moment is His, and we
are under the most solemn obligation to improve it to
His glory. Of no talent HE has given will He require
a more strict account than of our time."

Therefore, do not throw away your confidence, which
has a great reward. For you have need of endurance,
so that when you have done the will of God, you
may receive what was promised.
(Hebrews10:35–36)

Do not neglect the spiritual gift within you, which
was bestowed upon you through prophetic utterance
with the laying on of hands by presbytery. Take pains
with these things; be absorbed in them, so that your
progress may be evident to all. (1 Timothy 4:14)

One of my heart-felt desires was to visit all of the national parks in the continental United States. At the time of my plan to drive across the country, I had not visited any of the parks east of the Mississippi. My farthest destination from Santa Cruz, California, was traveling to Acadia National Park off of the coast of Maine. How in the world could I drive that far from home, all by myself? Of course, spiritually, I knew the Holy Spirit would be with me no matter what, so I let my anxieties go.

A few weeks into this plan of my desire, I got a phone call from Atlanta, Georgia. Somehow, a church out there had heard one of my songs on the Internet and they asked me to come out to them and sing in late June. Hum? I wonder? I prayed about it and then I kept asking if this was a reasonable way of spending my *time?*

Meanwhile, two additional training conferences came up for me to attend in the area of coaching and relationships. Both of them were in New Jersey about ten days apart and in the middle and end of July. That timing gave me a perfect opportunity to run up to Cape Cod and then on to coastal Maine for my pictorial nature and hiking fix in Acadia National Park.

One of my ministry couple friends had begun a new church four years prior in Venice, Florida. I had wanted to visit them as well. Lots to do on the east coast region along with my interest in the national parks. Their town was north and west from the Everglades and Biscayne National Parks. They lived along the gulf side of the Florida coastline.

One last desire was to visit the town of Sudbury, Ontario, in Canada where I had gone to school in the seventh grade. Yes, I absolutely had to go there because I knew that the town had grown to a reasonably good-sized city since then. Sudbury had become a significant cancer treatment and research center. I had worked in pharmaceutical sales for a cancer treatment medication that had been studied there and had heard of their progressive practices.

The municipality had grown from 80,000 or so to over 160,000 people and I had to see it again. Lots of fond memories in a composite of communities enmeshed with 300 small lakes and numerous rocky grounds. My hope was to see how this community had changed over the 50-some years since I had last been there.

Somehow, God made this desirable trip of mine a reality. The 66-day journey, time off from work and finances came together beautifully. God's timing brought singing opportunities in numerous churches on weekends and most of them were open to my last minute scheduling.

An unforgettable timing aspect of my trip happened as I came back from Canada. After crossing over the Sault Ste. Marie Bridge into northern Michigan, I called the modest motel to confirm my reservation for the night. They had tried to reach me earlier, however, I was unable to get their message due to a lack of international phone connection. I could not believe how everything was going so smoothly and now, I had no place to stay. Scampering about desperately, driving and looking for lodging on a Saturday night, resulted in no alternative places in the area for miles around.

I felt disappointed that nothing seemed to be opening up for me. Fortunately, I was able to convince the lodging site to allow me to at least spend the night in my car on their grounds. It was a far sight better than camping out in a tent, which I did not have anyway. How could I have overlooked this detail of my trip? I was really too tired to deliberate any longer so I just crashed in slumber.

As I slept soundly in my reclined car seat, the most startling roar of water awakened me. It came crashing down on my rooftop followed by a brief interruption so that I could see the veins of lightening blaze across the sky. This was by far the most incredible thunder and lightning storm I had ever seen. It continued for some length of time and I marveled.

Had I been sleeping anywhere else except under the protection of my windshield, I would have missed the most amazing show of lights. It was a spectacular display of Mother Nature's source of energy and seemed to have lasted longer than any rendition of celebratory fireworks I had ever known. Thank you, God. I have so learned to trust in His timing.

The Joy of Purpose

If you evaluate the four commandments as outlined above from Genesis 1:28 to Genesis 4:7, you may notice how the cycle begins and ends with living the purpose God created you for and abiding in Christ to see you through. The aspect of being fruitful and to multiply is a creative process. Likewise, the commandment given in Genesis 4:7, to master sin, is also a creative exercise. Christ is the master of all creativity, as stated in John 1:3, "All things came into being by Him, and apart from Him nothing came into being that has come into being."

As you abide in Christ, the way out will be revealed, as it says in 1 Corinthians 10:13, "No temptation has overtaken you but such as is common to man; and God is faithful, who will not allow you to be tempted beyond what you are able, but with the temptation will provide the way of escape also, so that you will be able to endure it." A more complete description of sin and its remedy through Christ is given in Chapter 6.

Rick Warren covers the concept of your purpose in his book, *The Purpose Driven Life.* The five areas of consideration he lists are: To be in relationship with God; To participate in His Family; To become like Christ; To be shaped for serving God; and To live for a Mission.

The important thing to remember is that you were not made to judge. Jesus has been given that assignment by God, John 5:22. In the human state one may judge, however, it is not the source of your joy.

When judgments take you off course, go back to the joy of contribution; find your fulfillment in service, and purpose, as outlined above. This is tied closely to the first commandment of God in Genesis 1:28, to "be fruitful and multiply." Doing something creative takes your mind and heart out of judgments. You were meant to give in the grand plan of life and implementing the desired action of contribution assures your health, vitality and joy.

One of the other difficulties associated with judgment is lack of forgiveness. How much time has been spent hoping and wishing for a better past? Forgiveness towards others, or even yourself, does not sanction the undesirable behavior. It does, however, free you of that bondage of time being used to rehearse the event or even consider retaliation. What can serve to release that bondage is letting God's sovereignty reign, trusting Him for vindication as it says in Psalm 35:27, Jeremiah 51:10 and Isaiah 54:17.

Prayer regarding the nature of the circumstance, as Jesus did on the cross, cannot be underestimated. In time, developing a sense of compassion and mercy for the perpetrator, including you, is a learned spiritual practice that will save time. It does not come easily.

This ability to exercise compassion is developed over time as you learn to trust God's plan daily. Much more could be said about forgiveness, however, for now it must be recognized as a characteristic of the mature Christian. You were born with a human nature that has its purpose. During the sanctification process, that human nature grows toward the Divine Nature of God.

Forgiveness allows you to move forward in your purpose. This source of joy is irreplaceable and a living testimony to your significance. God's character reflects your value as though you are the only one that matters. However, in your journey, there will be trials, challenges and setbacks. This is when attention to the vision is paramount. That vision, or "anchor in the night" must be held strong. These are faith-building opportunities and transformational pivot points that allow you to emerge as a stronger, more grounded, confident *new* you. This is why God gave you abilities and the desire to use them. They are designed to grow you into a higher version of yourself. This is the value of using your *time* on earth wisely and in the fulfillment of God's purpose for you as a human *being*.

CHAPTER FOUR

Time-Robbers

If I only had remembered
To keep my eyes on Him,
I would not be here wasting time
And seeing life so grim.

The stage of life is not a rehearsal.

In the pursuit of our dream vision, time-robbers are bound to emerge. These are easily recognized as less enthusiastic periods and often brought about by negative evaluations. These are the sources of bondage that become significant time-robbers:

TIME-ROBBER	BIBLICAL SOLUTION
Quick Anger	He who is slow to anger has great understanding, But he who is quick-tempered exalts folly. PV 14:29
Anger	So remove grief and anger from your heart and put away pain from your body, because childhood and the prime of life are fleeting. Eccl 11:10
Wrath	A gentle answer turns away wrath, but a harsh word stirs up anger. PV 15:1

TIME-ROBBER	BIBLICAL SOLUTION
Rescue	A man of anger will bear the penalty, for if you rescue him, you will only have to do it again. PV 19:19
Provocation	He who provokes him to anger forfeits his life. PV 20:2
Jealousy	"You shall not covet…" Ex 20:17 (and to remember that comparing is despairing)
Complaining	He made them wander in the desert 40 years. Num 32:13
Rushing	Only a few things are necessary, really only one, time with Me. Luke 10:42
Judgment	Do not judge lest you be judged. Matt 7:1
Over Commitment	Focus on the major things and give minor things to others to do. Ex 18:22
Unrest/Lack of Peace	So far as it depends on you, be at peace with all men. Rom 12:18
Lack of Forgiveness	Bless those who curse you, bless them and curse not. Rom 12:14
Regret	No one, after putting his hand to the plow and looking back, is fit the kingdom of God. Luke 9:62
Indecision	But let your statement be, 'Yes, yes' or 'No, no'; and anything beyond these is of evil. Matt 5:37

TIME-ROBBER	BIBLICAL SOLUTION
Making Decisions	In abundance of counselors is victory. PV 11:14
Discernment	The mind of man plans his way, but the Lord directs his steps. PV 16:9
Direction Question	Thy word is a lamp to my feet, and a light to my path. Ps 119:105
Lack of Faith	You meant evil against me, but God meant it for good in order to bring about this present result. Gen 50:20
Fabrications	"Why did you say, 'She is my sister,' so that I took her for my wife?" Gen 12:19 (about trusting God in the truth)
Procrastination/Disobedience	Book of Jonah
Pride/Arrogance	Do you see a man wise in his own eyes? There is more hope for a fool than for him. PV 26:12
Failure to Plan	The prudent man sees evil and hides himself, the naïve proceed and pay the penalty. PV 27:12
Peer Pressure	The fear of man brings a snare, but he who trusts in the Lord will be exalted. PV 29:25
Lack of Prayer	There is a way which seems right to a man, but its end is the way of death. PV 14:12

TIME-ROBBER	BIBLICAL SOLUTION
Misrepresentation	He who conceals his transgressions will not prosper, but he who confesses and forsakes them will find compassion. PV 28:13
Lack of Wisdom	But if any of you lacks wisdom, let him ask of God, who gives to all men generously and without reproach, and it will be given to him. James 1:5
Focus on Past	I forget what lies behind and reaching forward to what lies ahead, I press on toward the goal for the prize of the upward call of God in Christ Jesus. Phil 3:13–14
Pain of Change	Stripes that wound scour away evil, and strokes reach the innermost parts. PV 20:30
Impatience	Consider it all joy, my brethren, when you encounter various trials, knowing that the testing of your faith produces endurance. And let endurance have its perfect result, that you may be perfect and complete lacking in nothing. James 1:2–4
Disturbed by Imperfection	Finally, brethren, whatever is true, honorable, right, pure, lovely, whatever is of good repute, if anything worthy of praise, let your mind dwell on these things. Phil 4:8

TIME-ROBBER	BIBLICAL SOLUTION
Fear of Tomorrows	Give us this day our daily bread. Matt 6:11 So do not worry about tomorrow; for tomorrow will care for itself. Each day has enough trouble of its own. Matt 6:34
Guilt	I acknowledged my sin to You, and my iniquity I did not hide; I said, "I will confess my transgressions to the Lord"; And You forgave the guilt of my sin. Psalm 32:5

All of these sources of bondage impact the efficiency of *time*. They are the fulfillment of Satan's dream to throw you off track and help further discouragement. There is no glory in these behaviors and they interfere with lifting the problem into the solution phase. Each Biblical Solution listed above is a reminder of the character of God to implement your peace and joy. Remember the promises of a focus on the Kingdom, divine power and perfection from Jesus the Son, and how God is there to fight your battles. All of these resources help provide the way out. Trust in the *being*, as His beloved, and see the result you are looking for.

Once Upon a Time

Once upon a time, beautiful bedtime stories were written of people who lived happily ever after. These were stories of how the prince was able to wake up the sleeping beauty, find the right woman to try on the glass slipper, or have the maiden let down her hair so he could climb up to see her. That special time of triumph made amazing stories for children; however, in order to live happily ever after you must have good communication and responsibility skills. Living from the inner truth of your word is what counts. That means saying "Yes" when you mean "yes" and "No" when you mean "no" (Matthew 5:37).

Long-term relationships require spending quality time together and developing trust between each partner. Agreements must be reached regarding raising children, family time and budgeting. In fact, lawyers, therapists and accountants often cite financial difficulties as the cause of relationship break-ups. I believe money is important, but it is trumped by effective time and communication with one other. Time is a form of currency. It is vital to determine how the couple views time and its use to create their desired life as a team. Spending too much time apart without communication and responsible action is the foundation for disaster.

As a Christian seeking to grow in His likeness, a relationship with Jesus is where to start. The fruits of the Spirit serve as a way of determining success with this important relationship. Galatians 5:22–23 cites the fruits of the Spirit as love, joy, peace, patience or long-suffering, kindness, goodness, faithfulness, gentleness and self-control. Developing these abilities by your own effort or *doings* is cumbersome and short-lived. However, *time* in the Word, studying the life of Christ and His attributes, generates a likeness of His *being* in you. From that likeness the fruits emerge.

If you notice that you are not living in a place of love, joy, peace, patience or long-suffering, kindness, goodness, faithfulness, gentleness and self-control, chances are time alone in His Word studying the Bible has not been enough. Time is needed to solidify your relationship with Him and create the *being* that naturally produces the desired fruits and your divine nature. This is one of the most valuable uses of time and begins to create the heaven on earth that is available to you. These fruits of the Spirit combat the time-robbers of life. It is how once upon *this* time (in Bible study) allows you to live happily ever after.

Time Traps

Let us now look at another significant bondage to time associated with ancient interpretations that have arisen out of early childhood, adolescent or young adult years. I call these interpretations *time traps*. Along with the judgments and time-robbers listed above, there are times when people say hurtful things to you at an early age in life. Often what they say is simply a position that they hold for themselves, but it is interpreted as a direct affront to you that is not empowering.

An example would be that your mother and father decided to get a divorce and your father left to live in another city. That event could be interpreted as a form of rejection. As a result, you decide that you were not worthy of being loved enough to keep your parents together. Perhaps you felt that your father did not love you enough to even stay in the same city so that you could see him on a regular basis. In time, you developed a protective stance that people you love will abandon you because you are not enough, you are not lovable or any number of other possible interpretations.

In order to protect yourself, you decide that you will never allow anyone to hurt you that way again. You become distant with relationships, even with people who are in your age group. Alternatively, you may decide that since you are not worthy of being loved for who you are, you will immerse yourself into schooling, performance or your career to prove that you are truly enough based on accomplishments. As a result, relationships suffer over the years and you begin to experience loneliness, lack of communication skills or a host of other isolating behaviors to protect yourself. Notice the pattern of becoming a human *doing* instead of a human *being*.

As time goes by, and it may even be decades, you decide that life is not working. At some point, you discover or learn that the behavior of your parents was simply their need to make a choice for themselves and it had nothing to do with how much they loved you or your worthiness to be loved. That false interpretation, based on hurt feelings, kept you trapped from moving forward in a healthy way with your life for a considerable period of time. That is what I am referring to as a *time trap*. You have been trapped by a false story about a situation that happened many years ago. You decided to protect yourself from ever having that happen again, so you accepted the lie about yourself as the truth.

These time traps come attached to many interpretations of what actually happened verses what you decided it meant to you. What you believe to be the truth is based on how you felt at the time of the event. They become your *stories*. Situations of how a person may experience a hurt are, being rejected for a team or partner position, not getting the help that you need in a difficult life situation, or the hurt associated with unmet expectations.

Generally these hurts may be identified if you find yourself complaining habitually about a type of situation or event. The people or situations may change, but you have a pattern of being the same victim over and over again. The ego has a masterful capability of playing the role of "poor me" when it does not get what it expects. Undoing the bondage of these time traps may be overcome by isolating the past hurt, acknowledging the "truth" of that situation and shifting the energy of perspective. You must evaluate the need for forgiveness, compassion and/or communication, whether in person or in writing. All three may be required.

Going through the process of eliminating this bondage to time traps may require getting the help of a well-trained coach, counselor, prayerful insights with scripture or educational programs. Although looking deeply inside may be painful, it will markedly reduce future failure of endeavors and save you a lot of time in the long run. Can you think of a time when what you thought was happening was simply an untrue belief or interpretation that ended up keeping you stuck in a time trap?

The following story demonstrates how God can communicate important messages about *time* when we are struggling with what to do in a difficult situation.

My Discontent in Time

One of my godmothers wanted to go to South America in May of 2000. The trip involved participation in a research project of sea turtles with the Oceanic Society. It was her dream of celebrating her 70th birthday, and she asked me to join her. I was so busy with work and doing a lot of travel myself with corporate trainings and sales activities that the thought of a vacation sounded great. Unfortunately, I did not get very involved with the planning of the trip, which set me up for some unanticipated experiences.

I planned to go and had my passport ready to travel as her companion on her dream adventure. She was eagerly anticipating this trip. I, on the other hand, began feeling like a week at home might really be what I needed. It turned out that I was training a new sales associate in New Orleans, Louisiana, until the end of the week. I had to fly home to California before I could leave again for Miami the next day, and begin the journey to South America. That alone was a bit of a time crunch for me trying to process the jet lag back and forth over such a short period of time.

Our first travel day was flying from San Francisco to Miami and arriving on the east coast after 5:30 p.m. The one and only plane available to take us farther on our journey left every day at

4:30 p.m. so we had to wait until the next afternoon to leave the United States. This gave us a great opportunity to relax and just do some casual sightseeing.

We had a group of six other people from the United States that met us the next day when we all flew out of Miami on our way to Curacao, just north of Venezuela. The reason the flight could not go directly to Paramaribo, Surinam, was because American flights were not authorized to fly directly to that country. Unfortunately, the aircraft that was to have taken us to Paramaribo was experiencing some mechanical failures. We all had to wait several hours at the airport for another carrier to deliver passengers to Buenos Aires, Argentina, first. By the time that plane flew back to pick us all up and take us on the remaining hour and a half flight to Paramaribo, it was quite late.

We reached our destination in South America well after midnight. Our hotel was another hour drive by van in the dark. Enjoying the local scenery was impossible, but did generate some anticipation for the next day.

Once our group reconvened in the lobby the next morning, we visited some local sites and learned of the impending political events. We visited a food market with huge gondolas of meat and vegetables. The meat counter had what looked like large cuttings of sea turtle legs and thighs, although they claimed it was illegal to eat sea turtles. The capital city of Paramaribo was also preparing for a national election in a few days. We learned that the country had 17 political parties and that the incumbent president was being replaced because of financial mismanagement. There was an undertone of insurgence.

The afternoon entailed a tutorial on our research goals. Sea turtles are huge, over 700 pounds. They attract a lot of attention when they come up out of the water during the day, so the mother sea turtles would come up on shore to lay their eggs at night in order to protect the birthing of their young. We were to measure the sea turtles, notate where they were laying their eggs and how many. We were also given warnings regarding jungle safety with insects, snakes and drinking water. So far, the trip was interesting but not exactly the resort vacation that I had envisioned. Perhaps the research site would have a day spa or something that I could use to relax and just enjoy nature.

Research to the Rescue

The next morning our group of eight plus the research director and attendants took a jeep ride out to the coast of the Marowijne River on our way to the reserve. It was only seventy miles from Paramaribo, our starting point. The first 35 miles were composed of rugged roads loaded with potholes. We could not drive very fast at all. Apparently, that county did not appropriate funding for road maintenance. Once we hit the second county, the asphalt was fresh and smooth, much like we were accustomed to in the United States. However, they had constructed speed bumps every mile or so, in order that people would not drive too fast. It took all morning to get through those 70 miles in our jeeps.

By noon, we had arrived at the coast and relaxed with a meal of sustenance that essentially kept us from starving. From there, we embarked on two motor-driven canoes heading north towards the mouth of the river, which emptied into the Atlantic Ocean. As we approached the turtle reserve, the number and colors of opaque plastic motor oil containers that had been washed up from the riverbanks struck me. Apparently, there were no guidelines on what could be thrown overboard by passing boats. The mile-and-a-half long beach reserve was loaded with broken plastic chairs, aluminum cans, drinking bottles and glass. I began to feel so sorry for the mother turtles that had to use these grounds as their "labor and delivery room."

Once at the turtle reserve site, we were given the essential orientation of dos and don'ts. The highlight of the afternoon was excavating a turtle nest with late blooming hatchings. These baby turtles were no larger than the palm of your hand, but they were destined to develop their muscles for traversing the sand and then swimming all on their own. As the five babies were scaling the rugged sand pockets, one bird swept down and captured his lunch. The remaining tiny turtles finally made it to the water, however a hungry fish of some sort immediately snapped one of them up.

After an early dinner and sunset, we captured a few hours of sleep. By 10:30 p.m. we were decked with mosquito protection, clipboards, pencils and a measuring tape. Our turtle data collection process had begun. We had to minimize the use of flashlights, as it would scare off the mother turtles emerging from the river, looking for a place to nest. Fortunately for all parties, there was a full moon and clear skies to provide remarkably well-lit grounds. We counted, measured and observed the egg laying statistics of 23 turtles that night.

Newly hatched turtle huffing it over the moguls of sand on its way to the river.

Our activities were very busy and intense. If you can imagine being sure to account for all of the turtles that came up on shore, getting the data needed, fighting off the mosquitoes while entrapped in our insect protective masks and hats. The moonlight helped once we found the turtle, but sometimes we could not tell if the dark blob on the distant sand was a mother turtle or a pile of jungle growth. The running around in silence was almost comical, yet demanding. We worked in twos, and sometimes as singles just to keep up the pace. By 3:30 a.m. we were pretty much done and went in to catch up on sleep.

This was my fifth day of vacation and I was working harder than at my day job!

As I lay there trying to get to sleep after the night's romp with the turtles, I could not help thinking that I was in the wrong place at the wrong time. We were in a basic hut with twin beds, asphalt tile flooring and orange water coming out of the faucets. We had to drink, bathe and launder with bottled water that was scarce. It was swelteringly hot, even at night, and the bugs were relishing every opportunity of feasting on the new fodder we represented. I could see why we had to get a yellow fever vaccination before coming here.

I was struggling to get to sleep and knew that I needed to get some soon. Before long, I had drifted into dreamland. In my dream, I discovered that somehow, I had gotten myself home again to California. I was in the elevator of a medical office building in Santa Cruz. On my way up to the third floor to see some doctors that were devout users of my hepatitis treatment product, I got to thinking...

"Wait! I can't go into that office!"

I had already told them that I would be gone for two weeks out of the country, and they are going to wonder why I came back so soon. "No," I thought. "I cannot go in there. It would be too embarrassing for me to explain to them why I came back so soon."

Then it dawned on me. I had abandoned my godmother and she was alone without me. I needed to get myself back to South America. "Oh, no," I thought. "I am going to have to fly to Miami, wait a day for the next flight to South America. Then I am going to have to wait in Curacao for the plane to get back from Argentina. Airport layovers are so unfriendly and stark."

I felt panic encroach with all of the time that I would need to get back to Paramaribo. The van ride to the hotel in the middle of the night would be so dreary. I hated sightseeing in the dark…

Then the next day, I'd have to listen to the turtle tutorial again after doing the city tour in the morning. How boring. I'd have to take the jeep on the next day for 35 miles of bumpy road followed by smooth asphalt with speed bumps for another 35 miles. There went the subluxation in my back. I would have to eat lunch on the river shore before taking the canoe up the river to the turtle reserve site. I did not even know the language and with all of that travel by myself in a foreign country, what if I got lost?

The worst part was I had left my dear poor ol' godmother in South America all by herself. I couldn't believe I had just abandoned her like that. Oh, this was terrible. I wished I had never left…!

And then I woke up.

I was so glad that I was still in South America after all. I learned that I could deal with this unexpected tropical trip much better if I just changed my perspective…Philippians 4:11 reminded me to be content in all things. My dream helped me understand why.

The rest of the trip was amazing. What made things come together was, I asked for a "day" job. I was assigned to measuring the temperature of the sand at three different levels every 20 yards. As I scaled the riverbank, I also saw to it that all of the debris was collected and removed. This was far more fulfilling as a contribution to the reproductive cycle of sea turtles. I finally determined what God wanted me to learn. He helped me deal with my discontent and I understood why, in a dream. Has something like this ever happened to you?

CHAPTER FIVE

Living in God's Timing

I know I need to do it,
But darn it all, I blew it.
Why has this come upon me?
How will I e'r get through it?

There is always time to demonstrate love.

God's timing is impeccable. His precision is undeniable. He may seem to be late but He is always on time. God has a plan and it cannot be thwarted. 2Chronicles 16:9 reminds us, "The eyes of the Lord move to and fro throughout the earth that He may strongly support those whose heart is completely His." The Lord protects us and guards our comings and our goings, as it says in Psalm 121. How God decides to use your time may not always make earthly sense. Let us look at how God used people in the Bible who chose to surrender to His plan.

The Faith of Moses

The life of Moses reflects the use of God's timing to accomplish what was necessary. In preparing him as a leader, Moses was adopted and raised in Egyptian royalty and education during a time when the Israelite babies were being captured and killed. He spent 40 years in this preparation of leadership and education. He began to sense a call to serve the Israelites, his native people. He was full of head knowledge and sought to free them from the bond-age of Egyptian rule.

Then, due to a rash move of vindication, he killed an Egyptian, which led to 40 years of additional training in exile and hiding. These were humbling years of service to his family in the low profile of a wilderness. At 80 years of age, God called him to negotiate with the Pharaoh of Egypt to let His people go. At first he did not feel qualified, but God empowered him to leadership with his brother Aaron. Moses spent the last 40 years of his life leading the Israelites from Egypt through the wilderness on their way to the Promised Land.

Moses learned so much during his assignment given by God. During this time, he wrote the first five Books of the Bible, referred to as the Pentateuch. His close relationship with God lead to his guidance of the people, the delivery of the Ten Commandments and leadership qualities that are recognized even today. His life represents the faith of living in response to God's voice. How many people today think of their first 80 years as preparation for their true significance in God's glory?

King David in God's Court

David is known as a man after God's own heart. This is the David who became King in his later years after slaying the giant Goliath from the Philistines. He had his shortcomings by having committed adultery with Bathsheba and then leading her husband, Uriah, to death so that he could marry her. David, however, recognized his weaknesses. He repented and honored God with the many Psalms that he wrote.

David was also a man of war. God had him in battle for specific purposes, yet David longed to contribute by building the

Temple of Jerusalem. Solomon, David's son and a man of wisdom, was given the task of building the Temple instead. King Solomon was a man of peace and God had already chosen him to build the temple.

Noah, Abraham, Isaac, Jacob, Joseph and countless other Biblical individuals used their time on earth to fulfill God's plan. The secret to their recognition and success was imperfect submission and faith. Understandably, these individuals were not mired with deadlines. They simply took the required steps as new direction was revealed.

Prolonged Life to Glorify God

The story of Lazarus is an interesting example of God's glory through His timing.

Mary and Martha had beckoned Jesus to come and prevent the death of Lazarus. Jesus purposefully waited four days to demonstrate His ability to raise Lazarus from the dead. Had he come earlier, there might have been a question as to whether or not Lazarus had actually died. In John 11:11, Jesus proclaims that Lazarus had only fallen asleep and that Jesus would go and awaken him from sleep. Thus in John 11:25–26, Jesus tells us that He is the resurrection and the life such that whosoever believes in Him shall live even if he dies, and that those who live and believe in Him shall never die. Death in Christ is a time of sleep until He returns.

In Matthew 9:18–26, the young daughter of a synagogue official had been pronounced dead, and Jesus still came to her home. He defied reason and the convention of death by stating, "Depart; for the girl has not died but is asleep." He then took her by the hand and she arose.

The crucifixion of Jesus is another demonstration of the raising of the dead. Jesus was hung on a cross with a slow earthly death on a Friday afternoon. He spoke His last words—"It is finished"—after asking God the Father to forgive his persecutors for this vicious act of misdirected justice and murder. He was put in a tomb as His burial site where He had a Sabbath rest. Sunday He arose from the tomb. It was His resurrection day, the first day of the week and the first day of His last 40-day walk on earth before He returned to heaven. There He sits at the right hand of the Father and intercedes for us, Romans 8:34.

These Biblical accounts demonstrate that in His power, death to believers becomes a deep sleep of the soul. In each person mentioned above, Jesus was able to call these two deaths back into life. He claimed that they were asleep in faith. When Jesus returns, He will claim His own at the Second Coming. In 1 Thessalonians 5:14–16 states that Jesus died and rose again, and that God will bring with Him those who have fallen asleep in Jesus. When the Lord Himself will descend from heaven, the dead in Christ shall arise first.

A lifetime on earth may be conceivably short or long in terms of years. King Hezekiah, a descendant of King David, was on the verge of death. He asked for more years to continue being a faithful servant of God. God granted him an additional 15 years of life as is described in 2 Kings 20:1–11. In John 12:48, Jesus points out that we will be bound by our choices in the last day, therefore see that you use your time wisely.

Returning to life after apparent death has happened many times in our modern day. Books have been written and movies have been made to demonstrate these miracles. These stories defy modern science. Regardless of the perception, there is a purpose for these occurrences because they demonstrate that God has not completed the use of their time on our conscious earth. These occurrences serve to glorify Him.

My father was a determined man of Bulgarian descent. He had many struggles as an immigrant to America and loved his six children immensely. Having escaped from under the Communist rule after World War II, he had many difficulties in adapting to his new life in a free country, including learning a new language, finding work and making new friends.

During the years of establishing our family economically, his health deteriorated and he developed a life-threatening bleeding ulcer. At one point, the doctors had all but pronounced him as dead. He would have nothing of the sort, as he knew that God had given him a family to provide for. He defied the doctor's prognosis and went on to live another two decades, with God's grace. Those were the years he continued to provide for his family, teach us to be responsible children, see us finish school and move into adulthood. The blessings of his love were irreplaceable.

Your intentions in accomplishment are greatly enhanced by the grace of God to empower you. In John 15:5, Jesus points out that He is the vine and you are the branches.

He goes on to say that "he who abides in Me and I in him, he bears much fruit; for apart from Me you can do nothing." This declaration of Jesus ties back to the first "Geniacle" commandment in Genesis 1:28, where God asks us to be fruitful and multiply, and shows that having that relationship with Jesus matters.

Earlier in John 8:12 Jesus also says, "I am the light of the world. Whoever follows me will never walk in darkness, but will have the light of life." Paul echoes this in Ephesians 5:8–10 by saying, "You were once darkness, but now you are light in the world, walk as children of light, trying to learn what is pleasing to the Lord." The fruitfulness of your life depends on the level of goodness, righteousness and truth that is given in service. God wants your life to shine in Him, and He will fulfill His purpose in you to live your life out for His glory.

Finding Things

How long have you spent trying to find something that was misplaced? Or, how much time has been spent finding just the right item you thought you had to have? One evening, I had to host a teleconference as I drove home. With earplugs and a hands-free phone, I reached home just before the end of the phone call. I backed into the garage, unloaded the car, and put food into the refrigerator as we said our good-byes. That conference was on Phone A.

I also have Phone B, which I use as a backup in case I lose Phone A. However, I keep Phone B on silent mode. It also has my GPS, email access and weather conditions. In my haste and distraction, I completely forgot the moment I had set Phone B down. At the end of my call, Phone A was still attached to my ear with the headset, so I knew where that was. Hours later, I needed Phone B but could not remember where I had set it down. I spent hours looking for Phone B as I unpacked my travel bags, emptied the car seats and reorganized my office desk. No luck.

What was a person to do? It had to be somewhere but I was not about to lose any more *time* looking for it, so I went to bed. Deep down, I knew that God would show me where the phone was, in His *time*.

The next day, I realized that I had forgotten to take two small rocks out of the back of my car. I had brought them home from the beach to remind me of my trip away. I opened the hatchback, removed the rocks, and placed them on the shelf directly behind the car. There on the shelf was Phone B.

In day-to-day activities, I have lost track of so many things. For less important items, I have decided that time spent looking for them was not going to be productive. They usually show up later when I am doing or looking for something else. For more important items, I have discovered that a better use of time is to ask for "divine" guidance sooner. When I do that, the location of the lost item would be brought to mind, without spending valuable *time* looking.

* * * * * *

I am not the best shopper. I am not fond of shopping, looking for just the right color, size or style of anything. I dread trying to find a place to park. I prefer to walk whenever possible and fortunately, everything that is important to me is less than three miles away from home. I especially like walking to church.

I wanted walking shoes that matched one of my favorite outfits. My mother had knitted a sweater for me that was black with a red pattern on it. That sweater with a black skirt or pants was a perfect combination for warmth in walking to church on colder days. All I needed were those black shoes with red trim.

Soon after I had that desire for those stylish shoes, I was on my way along the railroad tracks when, on the ground in front of me, there was a pair of black walking shoes with red trim. "WOW!" I thought. "How did these get here?" Since I was going to church, I left them there. I thought perhaps the owner would come back to pick them up. If they were meant for me to take home, they would still be there on my way back several hours later.

Black Shoes with Red Trim found on the railroad tracks.

Returning from church, the shoes were still lying on the railroad tracks, so I brought them home. They had a little sand on them, but washed up nicely and were a perfect fit. Amazing outcome. This was an interesting "find" for me as I dislike shopping and it saved me a lot of *time*. It reminded me of Matthew 7:7, "Ask and it will be given to you; seek, and you will find; knock, and it will be opened to you." Perhaps I need to ask for things more often.

The Reward of God's Timing

You may have experienced some of the benefits of God's timing. God is always working, but you may not see it because it is so subtle. The following experience from my days in sales could not have been better orchestrated by anyone or anything else than the Creator of all blessings. I call it Divine Grace.

Our pharmaceutical company was entering into the treatment arena of HIV therapy. There was a huge international AIDS conference being held in Florence, Italy, in June of 1991. For some reason our company only wanted to send two sales representatives to Florence, one from the east coast and one from the west. I was the west coast candidate.

These types of conferences were not only highly regarded by the physicians treating AIDS patients, but it was a phenomenal opportunity for building personal business relationships with our doctors that were not used to relying on us for drug therapy expertise. I quickly set up dinner meetings with key HIV treaters, infectious disease experts and speaker/researchers in this area of our drug therapy protocols.

The interesting thing was, I had just gone to Florence, Italy, the year before to sing Verdi's Requiem with the World Festival Choir in Verona. The concert was spiced with the voice of Pavarotti as the tenor. After the concert we had opportunities to explore the rest of Italy. Florence and Rome were on the top of the list.

As I investigated the centuries of statues and artwork of Florence, I also had a chance to visit two of the most exclusive hotels that were located in that city. One of the hotels was The Excelsior Hotel and across the courtyard was The Grand Hotel. Both places were completely out of my financial league.

I had gotten quite familiar with Florence during this musical trip to Italy, so when the time came to set up a dinner meeting with these important doctors, I knew exactly where to make the reservations. I phoned over to The Grand Hotel and explained to them who I was and what I needed. They were very accommodating.

On the night of my intended dinner reservation, they were having a massive HIV rally with Elizabeth Taylor as the key spokesperson for the evening event. The traffic around the coliseum was so congested that all of my dinner guests were over an hour late.

At first I felt a bit abandoned. After all, I was no competition for Elizabeth Taylor. How could I blame them?

Then, as patience would have it, my first doctor showed up. He was a speaker/researcher from the Los Angeles area. He briefed me on the traffic, dearth of taxies and informed me that the other physicians, who were coming to dinner, were on their way.

As we chatted and shared the highlights of the international conference so far, the rest of the doctors began showing up. I was seated with my back to the door so that I could focus on my audience of dinner guests. They all were facing the entrance of the room.

As we were discussing medical and conference events, a deafening silence struck all of them. I had no idea what had drawn their focus away from our conversation. I turned around to see what had captured their attention and noticed a string of young ladies gloriously dressed followed by a tall, longhaired blond male. Hum… Who could that be?

Then the parade of dinner guests heading for the table just behind ours came to an end. The last person to enter the room was the most stellar sight I have ever seen in a human being. It was Elizabeth Taylor herself; she was dressed in a white pearl-zed, long-sleeved hourglass cocktail dress. The energy that she garnered from the room was astounding. Her group of eight dined discreetly and quietly all evening right behind my table. My group of doctors soon restored their breathing with mental faculties and continued in conversation.

I later discovered that Elizabeth Taylor and her party were staying at The Excelsior Hotel across the courtyard and had eaten there the night before. The Grand Hotel was the venue for her second night of dining before she and her party were to return home the next morning.

Recognized for His Timing

The next day at the conference, I received a note from one of my HIV treating physicians. It read: "Thank you for the lovely dinner and educational event at our meeting last night. And inviting Elizabeth Taylor was a nice touch!" This is the glory and blessing of God's timing. He knew what I needed to create a memorable evening for my new clients.

Have you ever noticed a miraculous synchronicity in your life that was not of your own making? I am sure that you have had similar experiences as the one shared above. Often God is doing things in a way that you do not see right away but He is still working behind the scenes and in His timing. This is why it is important to thank Him at all times, even though the results are not yet evident. Faith that He has your best interests in mind will reveal His miracles. He loves you too much to do otherwise.

Time for Creation

God's command to be fruitful and multiply was first declared on the Fifth Day of Creation, the Day of Fish and Fowl. I had an intimate experience with this concept in 2000 when I went down to Surinam, South America, with the Oceanic Society, as previously described. The Oceanic Society had their turtle reserve located on a mile and a half of sandy beach just before the mouth of the Marowijne River emptied into the Atlantic Ocean.

The turtles would hoist themselves upon the shore of the sandy riverbanks at night mostly to build their nests and lay their eggs every 90 days or so. Our first night in May of 2000, we counted 23 turtles that came down the river to lay eggs. We were there for a full week and each night had several turtles come out of the water for nesting, but not as many as our first night. Each batch of eggs would be from 150 to 200 eggs. Poachers would dig up these eggs for ritualistic purposes. The turtle reserve of the Oceanic Society offered some protection for them.

Once the baby turtles hatched, they would usually come out of their nests at night, again to avoid being seen for food by the birds. They would be guided from their sandy nests towards the ocean by the glimmer of light reflected from the water. In the ocean, the hatchlings became food for larger fish until they were 16 years of age, too large and hard shelled for predatory animals to fit them in their mouths. The adult turtles might weigh from 700 to 800 pounds and would also be hunted for food by humans. Their shells would be used for crafts and leather adornments. The skin would be used for purses and shoes. The turtle reserve was designed to not only study these turtles, but to give them a safer haven for continuing the species.

The mother leatherback and green turtles would lay thousands of eggs during their lifetime of up to 65 years of age. They were highly fruitful during their reproductive years and would lay eggs until their year of death. Interestingly, out of every one thousand eggs laid, only one female turtle would survive in years long enough to begin laying eggs herself. That is a fruitful life indeed.

Leatherback turtle laying eggs after carving out her nest.

CHAPTER SIX

The Eternity of God's Time

There is good anticipation
In the advent of His coming.
But the joy of celebration
Are rewards that come in loving.

Unconditional love is the sunshine
for seeds of growth.

One of my favorite people in life continues to tell me and others, "Who you are depends on who you know." That is such an encouraging comment. I can remember years ago when I was just beginning my career in pharmaceutical sales. I had so many new patterns to develop. I had to trade the posture of people chasing me down for advice on drugs when I worked in different pharmacies for me going after people to use my product. As a sales person, I had to get out there and convince doctors, pharmacists and patients that using the drugs I represented was the best way to go. That is when I learned how to deal with rejection.

Rejection and demonstrating value in my services was a big challenge. It took a long time before I gathered the courage, stamina and self-worth it took to stand my ground, knowing that I had something valuable to offer. What helped me so much was partnering with other sales people that had more experience than I had. They encouraged and energized me. They believed in me, and

I began to gain my own high-energy style of enthusiasm. It really helped to rub shoulders with sales people who had the abilities that I sought.

In real estate, it is all about location, location, and location. When it comes to relationships and sales, influence or motivation, it is timing, timing, timing. Usually, the desired timing is *now*. Buy it now. Win them over now. Do it now. God wants us in relationship with Him now! He is actually preparing us to be in relationship with Him for eternity. He is the one you really want to rub shoulders with to create your best life now. How is this going to happen?

Preparing for Eternity

These days there is so much to be said about the Law of Attraction and how you need to live your life at a higher vibration. People with an energetic and enthusiastic attitude are so attractive. They pick you up from the feelings of hopelessness and despair.

There is no higher vibration than God's love for us. That is what makes God so attractive. He loves you with an everlasting love. If only people could see this vital connection to their life. Know God.

At this point, God is a concept of the mind. You can only know Him by spending time with Him and seeing His miracles in your life. Even so, those miracles will not be experienced unless your mind is open to what those miracles have to offer. Witnessing His faithfulness is how He becomes a reality. Even God in the flesh, as Jesus was, did not register because people were not open-minded enough to see what He had to offer and what He represented. Are you leaving your miracles on the table?

Our worldly life is so distracting from the heavenly realms of eternity. Jesus tells us in John 11:25–26, "I am the resurrection and the life; he who believes in Me shall live even if he dies, and everyone who lives and believes in Me shall never die. Do you believe this?" Belief in His promise is an act of faith because you cannot see the evidence yet. The media does not support this intangible reality. Yet, Paul reports in 2Corinthians 5:1, "For we know that if the earthly tent which is our house is torn down, we have a building from God, a house not made with hands, eternal in the heavens." Living in eternity has no bondage to time, because you, like God, become timeless. On the earthly plane, your focus begins to *be* on time *less.*

How the NOW Works

Once I was in a head-on collision with another vehicle. No one was hurt physically, but the emotional anguish was devastating for both parties. I was at fault. I had to contend with the turmoil of a traffic ticket, a totaled car, insurance dealings and unanticipated expenses. To top it off, I was even afraid to get behind the wheel again. I was really shaken.

The details took an entire day just to transfer materials from the car I was driving to a rental car. I was 400 miles away from home. The only way that I could deal with this trial and by the grace of God was to think of just one tiniest moment at a time. This is what got me home and allowed me to drive with caution. Just one series of "now" after "now," or "one step at a time."

On the earthly plane, there are confines of time, however they do not need to bind you up to the levels of stress that exist today. Knowing that everything will truly happen in God's time is a bit of a relief. What is also sobering is that if it is truly important, God will see that it happens because He is ultimately in charge. He will see that it happens whether you do it or not.

A good question to ask when things do not go according to plan is, "Will this matter in eternity?" As a Christian on earth, it is not as though you are *now* timeless, as mentioned above it is that now you think of *time less*. In this way you are not living under the stresses associated with the bondage of time. You begin to experience life's events in God's perfect time as you progress to eternity.

How Jesus Does It

I have often heard the comment and read that Jesus is the unblemished Lamb. He knew no sin. What does it really mean to live without sin? Is it about obedience? Is it always saying the right things? Is it that that you do not spill your drink when you are at a barbeque? To answer this question, I look back into the Book of Genesis and what happened to Adam and Eve.

You have read that the serpent in the Garden of Eden deceived Eve. She ate the fruit from the tree of the knowledge of good and evil. God had already commanded Adam not to eat of this fruit, as this behavior would result in death. When the serpent told Eve that she could eat from that tree and still live, he planted a seed of doubt. When she ate the fruit and lived, she then went on to share the fruit with Adam.

Adam also ate of this fruit, based on Eve's invitation and knowing what God had commanded. Then realizing that they had been disobedient, they broke their trusted relationship with God. They hid from Him as He came to enjoy fellowship with them. They hid. They blamed. They did not take responsibility for their actions. They did not confess the truth of their choices. They did not realize that their actions of disobedience would lead to a separation from God. That separation from God is the "death" that God is referring to. That separation of relationship is *the* sin that must be laid aside, Hebrews 12:1, and *the* sin that results in transgression of the law. It is like being a plant that gets uprooted. It stays green for a while but withers away over time because it has lost its root connection to the source of life.

Separation from God is restored when one believes in the salvation God provided through Jesus. He is the one that pays for that sin of separation that was brought on by disobedience and unfaithfulness. It begins with a confession of disobedience and of faith that Jesus is the redemption for one's sin. It is the belief that Jesus is the savior. He allows you to restore that fellowship with God as was initially designed in the Garden. That is the source of true joy, true love and true life. Eternal life.

As it says in John 1:1–5:

> *In the beginning was the Word (Jesus the Word),*
> *and the Word was with God, and the Word was God.*
> *He was in the beginning with God. All things came*
> *into being by Him, and apart from Him nothing*
> *came into being that has come into being.*

In Him was life, and the life was the light of men.
And the light shines in the darkness,
and the darkness did not comprehend it.

So what people do not understand is that life is *with* God, the source. Jesus, the Word, is the opportunity to choose that life *with* God, His blessings, and His prosperity, His Truth, His Light and His Fellowship. God allows you to choose Him with your free will.

Why is this important? Jesus is the life. In John 8:12–13 He says, "You are from below, I am from above; you are of this world, I am not of this world. I said therefore to you, that you shall die in your sins; for unless you believe that I am He, you shall die in your sins."

In John 11:26 Jesus goes on to say, "And everyone who lives and believes in Me will never die. Do you believe this?" To never die is to live in eternity. If you are to live in the joy of eternity, you must love and enjoy fellowship with Jesus *now*. You are completely at choice.

Sin is the eternal separator in your relationship to God. Jesus is our salvation from that sin of separation. What would happen if you went from SIN to SON?

Separation from God In the NOW to Salvation Only in Jesus Now

Jesus is the redeeming connection to God. Jesus is God incarnate that walked on earth. If you look at John 5:30 Jesus says, "I can do nothing on My own initiative. As I hear, I judge; and My judgment is just, because I do not seek My own will, but the will of Him who sent Me."

What that says to a person such as myself is, I can do all kinds of things with my earthly intentions, but it will all come to nothing significant, because I was not using the seeds of God's will to implement my task. It is much like putting diesel fuel in an engine designed for unleaded gasoline. Things may work for a while, but then difficulties result.

So as you were given free will, you may choose not to run the program that you came to earth with and experience dis-ease, lack of joy and tiring frustrations. Or you can choose to turn your focus of time on earth into the joy that you were intended to live by your "design" engineer, God, the Creator.

If you look closely at your life and notice the struggles, ask yourself, "Am I doing this because I am supposed to do this or because I really want to do this?" Many individuals have adopted a worldly perspective of fame, fortune and/or accomplishment. These are individuals that have allowed worldly direction to dictate a worldly intention. On the other hand, Godly direction emerges from within such that what you do naturally brings you fulfillment, peace and prosperity. All of these benefits come to pass while you are simply living in the JOY of your Creator. This is what Jesus did, and allows you to do, when you abide in Him.

CHAPTER SEVEN

Choosing the Eternal Promise of NOW

There is now a precious minute
Only sixty seconds in it.
You can relish or consume it
Yet eternity is in it.

This moment is irreplaceably yours. Use it wisely.

If you remember, our discussion earlier was of the *second* being the universal measure of time. As *now* is the most frequently used measure of time in the Bible, perhaps it would be useful to consider this next point. At this very *second* you are united with every other person on this planet earth, regardless of time zones, culture or language. We all automatically have *this* second in common, this *second* called *now*. What would happen if you took advantage of that unity with every single other person on earth right *now*? To date that includes over seven billion people, kings, queens, presidents and leaders, rich and poor.

The collective energy of unity is invigorating and completely in the *now*. If you couple that with the understanding that in eternity there are no days, nights, weeks, months or years, as they are experienced on earth today. God exists in the eternity of *now*. What would happen to your conscious awareness if you remembered that now is all that counts? Not only are you united with the energy of earthly humanity, but you can experience the presence of God in eternity in that same *now*. It is the ultimate unifying possession that you have. Take a *second* and experience that right *now*. What is the energy that you are feeling with this thought? How long would you enjoy this energy in your present awareness? Eternity is simply a series of *nows*.

Regardless of how this experience is realized, choosing *now* has many remarkable benefits that energize, heal and exuberate. Choosing *now* is how you become a human *being*, not a human *doing*. Out of this being-ness, the doings simply flow effortlessly and without stress. It may take a while for you to develop the habit of this being-ness because it is an unfamiliar practice for most individuals. To assist in this practice of being, I have designed several aspects of choosing *now* that may be helpful. You may discover that *now* has quite a bit to offer, the more you practice this spiritual discipline.

Developing the Practice of NOW

I created this exercise to help in choosing *now*. These meditations may only take a minute of focus depending on how you would like to use them. Certainly, you may come up with other words of *now* that serve a specific use for yourself to focus on. As the appreciation of experiencing the present moment becomes more natural in your daily patterns and activities, a calming peace and open consciousness of God's grace will fill your spirit. This is the place that creativity, the genesis of joy, emerges from. It may be practiced all day long. This place of being allows a natural flow of energy to emerge. You will begin to do the exact and perfect thing that needs to be done with energetic enthusiasm. The ultimate goal would be to share that experience with another person and build from there.

For each of the opportunities to consider *now*, a Biblical verse is listed. Remember the breath of life that God breathed into His first living being. Use God's breath in you to magnify the experience of *now* with Him. Take one aspect of *now* each day, and review each attribute that is available in your quiet time. It does not need to be a long time each day, however, the attribute of *now* may be reconsidered throughout the day. If possible, read the context of the verse offered as a reference. Write down what thought each verse means to you. How can you apply this way of thinking each day, all day long? List any other verses that tie in with the daily consideration.

There are ninety-five perspectives of *now* that has been listed. They can be used in any order and some people use only two or three of their favorites. May they become thoughts and words that fill your default position of life each day. Soon your mind will gravitate to these aspects of *now* without laboring over the choice. They will become automatic.

This exercise focuses on the attributes of God that He has in store for you to experience, enjoy and share. It will allow you to understand and know God, your Creator, better. Living in these attributes *now* is designed to overshadow what the world chooses to report. Experiencing the presence of God throughout the day is what He designed you for. His protection, provision, empowerment and vitality are there for you to tap into. In time, you will experience a release from the bondage of time, energy and perspectives of judgment. Each moment of now will clarify the next moment going forward. You will live the JOY intended for your eternal life *now*. This is what heaven is all about, time with Him.

Staying in the NOW

THE PEACE OF NOW

Psalm 4:8 In *peace* I will both lie down and sleep,
for You alone make me to dwell in safety.

In this quiet moment alone, take a deep breath or two. Notice for yourself, how does *peace* come to you? There is nothing standing in the way of you and complete *peace,* except doubts of what God has already declared for you in His presence.

Thoughts _____

_____

Application_____

_____

Other Verses_____

_____

* * * * * * *

THE BEAUTY OF NOW

Psalm 96:6 Splendor and majesty are before Him,
Strength and *beauty* are in His sanctuary.

In this quiet moment alone, take a deep breath or two. Notice how there is *beauty* all around you. Life is truly *beautiful* and the more you notice the *beauty* all around you, the more *beauty* you will see. What do you see now that is *beautiful?*

Thoughts _____

_____

Application_____

_____

Other Verses_____

_____

THE FUTURE OF NOW

PV 23:18 Surely there is a *future*,
And your hope will not be cut off.

The *future* is built on the decisions of each now. Your *future* depends on what you are thinking and doing right now. You must be ready for your *future* in faith. Breathe into the eternal joy of knowing that you will be there based on these truths.

Thoughts _____

_____

Application_____

_____

Other Verses_____

_____

* * * * * * *

THE CHARM OF NOW

Song of Solomon 7:6 How beautiful and how
delightful you are, My love, with all your *charms*.

There is an inner delight in the *charm* of beauty all around. Close your eyes and breathe in this *charm* with peace, love and joy. It belongs to you in this moment. Know that you belong to God and He delights in you.

Thoughts _____

_____

Application_____

_____

Other Verses_____

_____

THE DISCIPLINE OF NOW

PV 23:12 Apply your heart to *discipline* and your
ears to words of knowledge.

Close your eyes and feel the flow of breath deeply into your lungs. Hold yourbreath for the count of four. Release the breath slowly. Repeat two more times. This *discipline* is energizing and prepares the mind to experience the presence of God quietly wherever you are. It opens the gateway to whatever needs to be done.

Thoughts _____

_____

Application_____

_____

Other Verses_____

_____

* * * * * * *

THE POWER OF NOW

PV 8:14 Counsel is mine and sound wisdom;
I am understanding, *power* is mine.

Breathe in deeply and feel the *power* that comes quietly with each breath. Close your eyes and know that the *power* of God is all around you. It is there to empower you as well. You can trust in the understanding that He loves you.

Thoughts _____

_____

Application_____

_____

Other Verses_____

_____

THE MERCY OF NOW

Jude 1:2 May *mercy* and peace and love
be multiplied to you.

In the quiet of a deep breath and closed eyes, see yourself completely loved and protected with divine *mercy*. Yes, there is plenty of *mercy* for God's beloved in Christ.

Thoughts _____

_____

Application_____

_____

Other Verses_____

_____

* * * * * * *

THE PATIENCE OF NOW

Colossians 3:12 So, as those who have been chosen by
God, holy and beloved, put on a heart of compassion,
kindness, humility, gentleness and *patience*.

You are on a divine journey that will never end. There is always room for improvement and yet you are preapproved in the process. Know that God is so *patient* with His work in you. Breathe in that *patience* to yourself and others, quietly.

Thoughts _____

_____

Application_____

_____

Other Verses_____

_____

THE GLORY OF NOW

Psalm 8:5 Yet You have made him a little lower than
God, and You crown him with *glory* and majesty.

Made in the image of God and living with others in community
also made in His image, you are learning new things. You are God's
highest creation and *glory*. Live in that space of creation that you
are made of.

Thoughts _____

_____

Application_____

_____

Other Verses_____

_____

* * * * * * *

THE WISDOM OF NOW

James 1:5 But if any of you lacks *wisdom*, let
him ask of God who gives to all generously and
without reproach, and it will be given to him.

The quiet time of this moment offers an opportunity to receive the
highest solution or answer to your question. Simply ask that powerful open question. Listen carefully to the *wisdom* that is freely given.

Thoughts _____

_____

Application_____

_____

Other Verses_____

_____

THE FREEDOM OF NOW

Galatians 5:1 It was for freedom that Christ set us
free; therefore keep standing firm and do not be
subject again to a yoke of slavery.

You were meant to live in the *freedom* of truth. Stand in that truth
for *freedom*. It was given to you for a purpose of glorifying the gifts
given to you by God for His glory. Freely give those gifts and find
the peace in that *freedom*.

Thoughts _____

_____

Application_____

_____

Other Verses_____

_____

* * * * * * *

THE GODLINESS OF NOW

1 Timothy 2:2 …so that we may lead a tranquil
and quiet life of *godliness* and dignity.

In the presence of God, now there is peace and tranquility. Take
that tranquility and dignity with you all day long. It is yours to
experience with joy and *godliness*.

Thoughts _____

_____

Application_____

_____

Other Verses_____

_____

THE RESULT OF NOW

James 1:4 And let endurance have its perfect
result, so that you may be complete and perfect,
lacking in nothing.

You are the *result* of all that has transpired in your life thus far. There is no judgment, simply God's love. Rest in the knowing that all is as it needs to be and that the best is yet to come in His presence.

Thoughts _____

_____

Application_____

_____

Other Verses_____

_____

* * * * * * *

THE JOY OF NOW

1John 1:4 These things we write,
so that our *joy* may be made complete.

Think of how much true eternal *joy* is in your life right now. *Joy* is the place of completeness. *Joy* is a choice that comes from knowing that God loves you and wants you continually seeking Him. You are His *joy*.

Thoughts _____

_____

Application_____

_____

Other Verses_____

_____

THE PERFECTION OF NOW

Ezekiel 28:12 'Thus says the Lord God, "You had the seal
of *perfection*, full of wisdom and perfect in beauty."

What would happen in your life if you thought of yourself as sealed
in God's *perfection*? What is standing in the way of this empowering thought? God created you full of wisdom and *perfect* in beauty.
That *perfection* is made *perfect* in Christ.

Thoughts _____

_____

Application_____

_____

Other Verses_____

_____

* * * * * * *

THE TRUTH OF NOW

Ephesians 4:24 …and put on the new self, which in the
likeness of God has been created in righteousness and
holiness of the *truth*.

There is a *true* self that is the essence of who you are. What do you
do to stay in touch with the righteousness of you? How does the
holiness of this *truth* portray itself in your daily activities? Trust
that your focus on Jesus is that source.

Thoughts _____

_____

Application_____

_____

Other Verses_____

_____

THE COMPASSION OF NOW

Psalm 106:46 He also made them objec*t*s of *compassion* in the presence of all their captors.

The love of God is seen in His *compassion* for you. He understands your every trial. What would you like to do to experience more *compassion* towards others, knowing that they have many trials in their lives also?

Thoughts _____

_____

Application_____

_____

Other Verses_____

_____

* * * * * * *

THE REJOICING OF NOW

Zephaniah 3:17 The Lord, your God is in your midst, A victorious warrior; He will exalt over you with joy; He will be quiet in His love, He will *rejoice* over you with shouts of JOY.

How delighted God is with you as He seeks your attention in relationship. He vindicates on your behalf those who have persecuted you. He is eternal and He seeks to share that eternity with you in joy. How can you *rejoice* in His love and exaltation and then share this with someone that needs light on their darkness?

Thoughts _____

_____

Application_____

_____

Other Verses_____

_____

THE SENSE OF NOW

Hebrews 5:14 But solid food is for the mature, who because of practice have their *senses* trained to discern good and evil.

Knowing what to do at the proper time is embedded deep inside through wisdom and comes to your awareness as doing righteousness. There is an internal compass that directs your *sense* of right and wrong. You use it wisely.

Thoughts _____

_____

Application_____

_____

Other Verses_____

_____

* * * * * * *

THE LOVE OF NOW

1 Corinthians 2:9 …but just as it is written, "Things which eye has not seen and ear has not heard, And which have not entered the heart of man, All that God has prepared for those who love Him."

God's *love* is eternal and He loves to bestow His *love* in so many ways. You cannot even begin to imagine the mystery of God's *love* for you. That *love* for you is given first, that you might know the power of *love* you can give to others. Your *love* for God can only grow as you see His *love* each day in your life.

Thoughts _____

_____

Application_____

_____

Other Verses_____

_____

THE GRACE OF NOW

Ephesians 2:8–9 For by *grace* you have been saved through faith; and that not of yourselves, *it is* the gift of God; not as a result of works, so that no one may boast.

Grace is God's freely given gift that cannot be earned. This mystery of God can be difficult to understand because it is not a worldly concept of cause and effect. The most effective thing to do with *grace* is appreciate it moment by moment and give it freely to others so they may see God's work in you.

Thoughts _____

_____

Application_____

_____

Other Verses_____

_____

* * * * * * *

THE VOICE OF NOW

Revelation 3:20 Behold, I stand at the door and knock; if anyone hears My *voice* and opens the door, I will come in to him and will dine with him, and he with Me.

To hear the *voice* of God is a powerful experience. He seeks to be in constant communication with you and His *voice* is full of wisdom and grace.

Thoughts _____

_____

Application_____

_____

Other Verses_____

_____

THE FORGIVENESS OF NOW

Matthew 6:12 And *forgive* us our debts,
as we also have *forgiven* our debtors.

Forgiveness is a powerful tool that releases a bondage of time and spirit. God *forgives* you as you recognize and confess your transgressions. You are released from the weight of that transgression and you get to start fresh. *Forgiving* others also frees you from ill feelings that block the flow of love.

Thoughts _____

_____

Application_____

_____

Other Verses_____

_____

* * * * * *

THE PRESENCE OF NOW

Psalm 21:6 For You make him most blessed forever; You
make him joyful with gladness in Your *presence*.

God's comfort and provisions, His love and compassion bring gladness to this moment. Experiencing His *presence* brings you to a valuable place of *presence* with yourself. It is indeed the moment of "now" for you in Him.

Thoughts _____

_____

Application_____

_____

Other Verses_____

_____

THE PRAYER OF NOW

Psalm 5:3 In the morning, O LORD, You will hear
my voice; In the morning I will order my *prayer* to
You and eagerly watch.

God always hears your *prayer* and He is always available to listen to
you. What is on your heart today to tell Him? Something exciting?
Something sad?He rejoices in hearing from you, knowing that you
have faith in Him.

Thoughts _____

_____

Application_____

_____

Other Verses_____

_____

* * * * * * *

THE CONFIDENCE OF NOW

Hebrews 4:16 Therefore let us draw near with *confidence*
to the throne of grace, so that we may receive mercy and
find grace to help in time of need.

Your *confidence* is very important to God. From the Greek, *confidence* means "with faith." God wants you to depend on Him with
faith. That is what He thrives on in His relationship with you.
Breathe into His *confidence* for you.

Thoughts _____

_____

Application_____

_____

Other Verses_____

_____

THE AWARENESS OF NOW

Isaiah 43:19 Behold, I will do something new, now it will spring forth; Will you not be *aware* of it? I will even make a roadway in the wilderness, rivers in the desert.

God is always at work in your world. Would that you could be *aware* of what He is doing for you right now. Knowing that you may miss something, what do you think might happen if you simply thanked Him at all times?

Thoughts _____

_____

Application_____

_____

Other Verses_____

_____

* * * * * * *

THE ACCEPTANCE OF NOW

1 Timothy 4:8–9 …godliness is profitable for all things, since it holds promise for the present life and also for the life to come. It is a trustworthy statement deserving *acceptance*.

The godly life is a spirit filled life. It is a life that *accepts* God's sovereignty in all things. You can trust that whatever God puts in place is worthy of *acceptance*.

Thoughts _____

_____

Application_____

_____

Other Verses_____

_____

THE SHADOW OF NOW
Psalm 17:8 Keep me as the apple of the eye;
Hide me in the *shadow* of Your wings.

God is so powerful, even His *shadow* bestows protection. You are the apple of His eye. Why would He allow anything evil to come upon you? Trust that His *shadow* is your safe and welcomed hiding place now.

Thoughts _____

_____

Application_____

_____

Other Verses_____

_____

* * * * * * *

THE SPIRIT OF NOW
Zachariah 4:6 "Not by power, nor by might but
by My *Spirit*." Says the Lord of hosts.

How can something so invisible be so powerful? His *Spirit* is the Nature and Mystery of God. What you see is temporary, but what you do not see is eternal. You know that God is working because you see the evidence of His *Spirit* now.

Thoughts _____

_____

Application_____

_____

Other Verses_____

_____

THE FEARLESSNESS OF NOW

Psalm 27:1 The LORD is my light and my salvation; Whom shall I *fear*? The LORD is the defense of my life; whom shall I dread?

Knowing that you and God are a majority, how will that impact what you do today? You can trust His voice of direction. You can count on His presence with *fearlessness*. You can know that His protection surpasses all things.

Thoughts _____

_____

Application_____

_____

Other Verses_____

_____

* * * * * * *

THE KNOWING OF NOW

Romans 5:3 And not only this, but we also exult in our tribulations, *knowing* that tribulation brings about perseverance

Life brings many trials and tests of your faith. You are being tested in order to emerge with your own testimony of God's plan in your life. What would happen if you *knew* that your trial is wrapped in His victory now?

Thoughts _____

_____

Application_____

_____

Other Verses_____

_____

THE PATH OF NOW

PV 4:26 Watch the *path* of your feet,
and all your ways will be established.

Every road goes somewhere. Stepping on that *path* results in a destination that lies at the end of that *path*. What *path* are you on right now that will truly bring you to where you want to go?

Thoughts _____

_____

Application_____

_____

Other Verses_____

_____

* * * * * * *

THE SIMPLICITY OF NOW

2Corinthians 11:3 But I am afraid that, as the serpent
deceived Eve by his craftiness, your minds will be led
astray from the *simplicity* and purity of devotion to Christ.

There is a *simple* way to create your joy. That joy is a promise from eternity to eternity. It is *simple* and yet not easy. God is there to strengthen you in any weakness now. How can you *simply* trust Christ for today's joy?

Thoughts _____

_____

Application_____

_____

Other Verses_____

_____

THE HARMONY OF NOW
Philippians 4:2 …live in *harmony* in the Lord.

Like music to your ears, *harmony* enhances relationships. In this moment, what song of life would you like to enrich with *harmony*? Having a common basis for appreciation and respect will bring any relationship to the gift God intended it to serve. You are built up now by the *harmony* that you create in the Lord.

Thoughts _____

_____

Application_____

_____

Other Verses_____

_____

* * * * * * *

THE CREATION OF NOW
Genesis 1:1 In the beginning God *created* the
heavens and the earth.

All that you see had a *creative* first beginning. Now is the perfect time to *create* something new. Your thoughts are the beginning of the new you or thing that you want to *create*. This is a godly concept brought to you by your Creator.

Thoughts _____

_____

Application_____

_____

Other Verses_____

_____

THE GROWTH OF NOW

1Corinthians 3:7 So then neither the one who plants nor the one who waters is anything, but God who causes the *growth*.

Growth is not easy, usually because it involves change and you are a creature of habit. One of the reasons that *growth* becomes difficult is because you are not in control of the process. We can only plant the seeds that are necessary to head in the right direction and God allows those seeds to sprout. Trust in this process as you focus on Jesus now and enjoy. Knowing Him allows you to *grow* in Him.

Thoughts _____

_____

Application_____

_____

Other Verses_____

_____

* * * * * * *

THE BLESSINGS OF NOW

Psalm 21:3 For You meet him with the *blessings* of good things; You set a crown of fine gold on his head.

What do all of the *blessings* around you look like? What would your life be like knowing that all you are is all that you need already? Why strive for what is only temporary? The eternal crown of glory in His blessings is already yours now.

Thoughts _____

_____

Application_____

_____

Other Verses_____

_____

THE ANSWER OF NOW

Psalm 38:15 For I hope in You, O Lord; You will answer

Your life is a reflection of the questions that you ask. The *answers* to those questions are what you see around you. How would you like to change your life? The *answer* requires you to ask Him a new type of question now.

Thoughts _____

_____

Application_____

_____

Other Verses_____

_____

* * * * * * *

THE ETERNITY OF NOW

Psalm 90:1 Lord, You have been our dwelling
place in all generations.

Eternity has no night or day, no minutes or hours. Your time with God is simply in the *now*. Practice the experience of the present moment and be prepared for the *eternal* time with Him in His dwelling place.

Thoughts _____

_____

Application_____

_____

Other Verses_____

_____

THE BREATH OF NOW

Job 33:4 The Spirit of God has made me, And the
breath of the Almighty gives me life.

When God breathed the *breath* of life into the nostrils of man,
the man became a living being. You cannot take another *breath* on
your own without the power of life that is given to you by God.
Breathe in His life now and live.

Thoughts _____

_____

Application_____

_____

Other Verses_____

_____

* * * * * * *

THE HEART OF NOW

Psalm 7:10 My shield is with God, Who saves the
upright in *heart*.

Your *heart* is the seat of your desires that were given to you by God.
Living in the *heart* of love for those godly desires is what God wants
you to protect and express, with His shield of faith. Breathe into
your *heart* now your desired life in Christ.

Thoughts _____

_____

Application_____

_____

Other Verses_____

_____

THE THOUGHT OF NOW

Psalm 139:2 You know when I sit down and when I rise
up; You understand my *thought* from afar.

Your *thoughts* are powerful and you get to choose them. From a distance God knows your deepest *thoughts* and understands them better than you do. Hold every *thought* captive to your highest good and you will see them materialize before your very eyes. Breathe into your *thoughts* in Christ now.

Thoughts _____

_____

Application_____

_____

Other Verses_____

_____

* * * * * * *

THE FLOW OF NOW

PV 4:23 Watch over your heart with all diligence,
For from it *flow* the springs of life.

How does the *flow* of life look to you right now? Where is the resistance coming from? Know that your life was designed to *flow* smoothly like the love that is bathing you from above. This is the flow of love that fills your heart and gives you the life God intended you to enjoy. Feel the *flow* of your life now.

Thoughts _____

_____

Application_____

_____

Other Verses_____

_____

THE RIGHTEOUSNESS OF NOW

PV 21:3 To do *righteousness* and justice is desired
by the LORD more than sacrifice.

As you breathe in deeply, know that this moment is filled with your *righteousness* in God's presence. He delights in your steadfast desire to please Him. You also rejoice in knowing that His justice is there to preserve your relationship with Him.

Thoughts _____

_____

Application_____

_____

Other Verses_____

_____

* * * * * * *

THE APPRECIATION OF NOW

Hebrews 12:28 Therefore, since we receive a kingdom which
cannot be shaken, let us show *gratitude*, by which we may
offer to God an acceptable service with reverence and awe;

Closing your eyes and breathing deeply, see the beauty of God's love, provisions and joy. His creation alone is the foundation of your existence. All that you have and know came from Him. Simply *appreciating* all of this is the highlight of His relationship with you.

Thoughts _____

_____

Application_____

_____

Other Verses_____

_____

THE BIRTH OF NOW

Ecclesiastes 3:2 A time to give *birth* and a time to die; A
time to plant and a time to uproot what is planted.

There is wisdom in renewal. Often you must discard or terminate
something that is outdated or broken to make room for the new
life you seek to live and be in. The *birth* of a new relationship with
yourself requires you to discard old habits and even relationships
that no longer serve your highest good.

Thoughts _____

_____

Application_____

_____

Other Verses_____

_____

* * * * * * *

THE FULLNESS OF NOW

Romans 15:29 I know that when I come to you, I
will come in the *fullness* of the blessing of Christ.

As you breathe into this new moment, close your eyes and see yourself fully present in the *fullness* of who you were meant to be by
God. See yourself taking that *fullness* into every moment of your
being right now. Breathe deeply again.

Thoughts _____

_____

Application_____

_____

Other Verses_____

_____

THE SONG OF NOW

1 Chronicles 13:8 David and all Israel were celebrating before
God with all their might, even with songs and with lyres,
harps, tambourines, cymbals and with trumpets.

Breathe deeply into the joy of this moment such that a *song* my
come out from your heart. A *song* is an expression of celebration
and victory. It is from this place that life begins anew with energetic
desire in goodness for your God given life.

Thoughts _____

_____

Application_____

_____

Other Verses_____

_____

* * * * * * *

THE TRANSFORMATION OF NOW

2 Corinthians 3:18 But we all, with unveiled face, beholding as
in a mirror the glory of the Lord, are being transformed into the
same image from glory to glory, just as from the Lord, the Spirit.

In a life of growth and *transformation,* your change is not of your
will but of His will for you as you focus on who HE is. This new
sense of being is brought about by your dedicated trust in knowing
your maker.

Thoughts _____

_____

Application_____

_____

Other Verses_____

_____

THE LEADING OF NOW

2Corinthians 7:10 For the sorrow that is according to the will of God produces a repentance without regret, *leading* to salvation, but the sorrow of the world produces death.

There will often be regrets for past indiscretions, yet you are not your mistakes. Christ forgives us and you are *led* to righteousness with a new spirit of understanding. Rest in that leading trust with faith. It will serve you.

Thoughts _____

_____

Application_____

_____

Other Verses_____

_____

* * * * * * *

THE REDEMPTION OF NOW

Ephesians 1:7 In Him we have *redemption* through His blood, the forgiveness of our trespasses, according to the riches of His grace.

You will miss the mark repeatedly and yet God loves you through it all and with the grace of Christ, He provided for your inevitable misdeeds. What is important is to recognize, learn and move forward with courage and the *redemption* of His blood. Breathe in the new life you have each day now.

Thoughts _____

_____

Application_____

_____

Other Verses_____

_____

THE SHELTER OF NOW

Psalm 5:11 But let all who take refuge in You be glad, Let them ever sing for joy; And may You *shelter* them, That those who love Your name may exult in You.

How can you fear when you have the love of God to protect and provide, *shelter* and secure you? This is not a small feat, and yet it may be difficult to see and receive as God has intended it to be for you. Breathe in the love and protection of Him.

Thoughts _____

_____

Application_____

_____

Other Verses_____

_____

* * * * * * *

THE CONTENTMENT OF NOW

1 Timothy 6:6 But godliness actually is a means of great gain, when accompanied by *contentment*.

It is blessed to be godly and yet it is a process that continues throughout life. As the process is unfolding, *contentment* with that progress is paramount, knowing that God calls you to Him just as you are and yet loves you too much to keep you that way. Breathe in His love with *contentment*.

Thoughts _____

_____

Application_____

_____

Other Verses_____

_____

THE ABIDING OF NOW

John 15:4 *Abide* in Me, and I in you. As the branch
cannot bear fruit of itself unless it *abides* in the vine, so
neither can you unless you *abide* in Me.

What greater connection could there be than connection to the
divine? You have such blessings in His family and all your days can
be filled with His fruitfulness. As the breath of life *abides* in you,
may you delight in His peace and productivity.

Thoughts _____

_____

Application_____

_____

Other Verses_____

_____

* * * * * * *

THE CONVERSION OF NOW

Acts 13:43 When the congregation was dismissed, many
of the Jews and devout converts to Judaism followed Paul
and Barnabas, who talked with them and urged them to
continue in the grace of God.

You have the power of the Holy Spirit to convict and *convert* you
to the joy of the truth. Walk in it with assurance of righteousness.
Rest in the truth of your Lord.

Thoughts _____

_____

Application_____

_____

Other Verses_____

_____

THE COMMISSION OF NOW

Colossians 1:25 I have become its servant by the *commission* God gave me to present to you the word of God in its fullness—

Living in the joy of His presence has resulted in such vitality and peace. How can you share that experience with others as you have been *commissioned* to by the Holy Spirit? Your experience deserves to be given to others as you have also had it given unto you.

Thoughts _____

_____

Application_____

_____

Other Verses_____

_____

* * * * * * *

THE TEMPLE OF NOW

Acts 17:24 The God who made the world and
everything in it is the Lord of heaven and earth
and does not live in *temples* built by human hands.

The Lord seeks a sacred place of communion with you. Your body is the *temple* of the Holy Spirit and thus you must take care of your body. Honor it in joy and peace. Breathe into it the breath of life from God and feed it the bread of life from Jesus Christ. You were made in the image of God. Embrace it now.

Thoughts _____

_____

Application_____

_____

Other Verses_____

_____

THE LIGHT OF NOW

1Corinthians 4:5 Therefore judge nothing before the appointed time; wait until the Lord comes. He will bring to *light* what is hidden in darkness and expose the motives of the heart. At that time each will receive their praise from God.

Assumptions and judgments can demolish your joy. Know that the *light* of truth will come forward and then live in it. Trust that light that is revealed to you.

Thoughts _____

_____

Application_____

_____

Other Verses_____

_____

* * * * * * *

THE UNITY OF NOW

Colossians 3:14 Beyond all these things put on love, which is the perfect bond of *unity*.

In this moment feel the *uniting* presence of God's love. We are all His work in progress. Together you can do so much more with the collaboration of all the gifts God has provided. This spirit of *unity* empowers you to go forward.

Thoughts _____

_____

Application_____

_____

Other Verses_____

_____

THE GREATNESS OF NOW

1Chronicles 29:11 Yours, Lord, is the *greatness* and the
power and the glory and the majesty and the splendor, for
everything in heaven and earth is yours. Yours, Lord, is
the kingdom; you are exalted as head over all.

Oh to know the *greatness* of the Lord. You have access to that *greatness* as heir in Christ. By association you will benefit from knowing Him. This is the heavenly gift of *greatness* through inheritance. Accept it now.

Thoughts _____

_____

Application_____

_____

Other Verses_____

_____

* * * * * * *

THE JUSTICE OF NOW

Psalm 25:9 He leads the humble in *justice*, And
He teaches the humble His way.

Humility is the virtue of complete surrender to the glory of God in your life. You do not need to fight to acquire *justice*. God will provide the confidence of truth to deliver *justice* and fight your battles for you. Stand firm in His *justice*.

Thoughts _____

_____

Application_____

_____

Other Verses_____

_____

THE DREAM OF NOW

Numbers 12:6 He said, "Hear now My words: If there is a prophet among you, I, the Lord, shall make Myself known to him in a vision. I shall speak with him in a *dream*."

There is a vision, a *dream,* of what God has made you to be and do. He clarifies His *dream* for you so that you may know His vision of your purpose. Heed with care His message to you in the quiet moments of now.

Thoughts _____

_____

Application_____

_____

Other Verses_____

_____

* * * * * * *

THE HEARING OF NOW

1John 5:14 This is the confidence which we have before Him, that, if we ask anything according to His will, He *hears* us.

Hearing is one of God's most compassionate attributes. As you speak to Him you will know what to ask for and how to use the information that He provides. This is the confidence of His message in His presence now.

Thoughts _____

_____

Application_____

_____

Other Verses_____

_____

THE FORTUNE OF NOW

Zephaniah 2:7 For the LORD their God will care
for them and restore their *fortune*.

This quiet moment of now may bring to mind lost opportunities, relationships, lost time or possessions. These losses were sent as teachers of His redeeming attributes. Loss is the gateway to new beginnings, new perspectives and new ways of living. Breathe in the *fortune* you have now.

Thoughts _____

_____

Application_____

_____

Other Verses_____

_____

* * * * * * *

THE HUNGER OF NOW

Matthew 5:6 "Blessed are those who hunger and thirst for
righteousness, for they shall be satisfied…"

Seeking righteousness with a *hunger* is all the more rewarding when satisfied. The righteous fulfillment of your purpose of love in service is where true joy of life stems from. Feel how that longing and *hunger* are satisfied now.

Thoughts _____

_____

Application_____

_____

Other Verses_____

_____

THE PROSPERITY OF NOW

Psalm 37:11 But the humble will inherit the land
And will delight themselves in abundant *prosperity.*

Breathe in the *prosperity* of now. Close your eyes and see the inheritance of eternal blessings that can never be taken away. Delight in the abundance of gratitude that you have for all that God has provided for you now.

Thoughts _____

_____

Application_____

_____

Other Verses_____

_____

* * * * * * *

THE SHARING OF NOW

Hebrews 13:16 And do not neglect doing good and
sharing, for with such sacrifices God is pleased.

A life of joy and abundance is what you can *share. Sharing* magnifies the value of the experience and enhances the lives that you touch. God is a giving God and serves as an example for all to follow. You are *sharing* this moment with God in the joy of His presence and delight. Seek to share.

Thoughts _____

_____

Application_____

_____

Other Verses_____

_____

THE BEST OF NOW

Acts 24:16 In view of this, I also do my *best* to maintain always a blameless conscience both before God and before men.

Breathe in the presence and holiness of God and know that you are doing your *best* with the knowledge and experience that you have acquired up until now. This does not mean that God is finished with you yet. You now live with the highest intentions of mastery through Him.

Thoughts _____

_____

Application_____

_____

Other Verses_____

_____

* * * * * * *

THE BEING OF NOW

Psalm 51:6 Behold, You desire truth in the innermost *being*, and in the hidden part You will make me know wisdom.

Your *being* is the essence of who God made you to be and He loves you in the process of your becoming. His wisdom is available to you as your unique self because you are a one-of-a-kind original, worthy of truth in Him.

Thoughts _____

_____

Application_____

_____

Other Verses_____

_____

THE NEWNESS OF NOW

Romans 6:4 We were therefore buried with him through baptism into death in order that, just as Christ was raised from the dead through the glory of the Father, we too may live a *new* life.

There is nothing better than the opportunity to start fresh, and yet benefit from past experiences that you might have wished never happened. This moment is *new*. God remembers your past no more. Why should you? Breathe that in.

Thoughts _____

_____

Application_____

_____

Other Verses_____

_____

* * * * * * *

THE TREASURE OF NOW

2Corinthians 4:7 But we have this *treasure* in jars of clay to show that this all-surpassing power is from God and not from us.

You are God's *treasure*. He made you and you are His. Relish the glory of this truth and live in it. Let this inspire you to be all of who you are with confidence.

Thoughts _____

_____

Application_____

_____

Other Verses_____

_____

THE GIFT OF NOW

John 4:10 Jesus answered her, "If you knew the *gift* of God and who it is that asks you for a drink, you would have asked him and he would have given you living water."

The *gift* of God's presence is the highest *gift*. In Him, through Him and with Him all things are possible for you. Breathe in that presence and enjoy.

Thoughts _____

_____

Application_____

_____

Other Verses_____

_____

* * * * * * *

THE BALANCE OF NOW

Proverbs 16:11 Honest scales and *balances* belong to the Lord; all the weights in the bag are of his making.

God wants you to live a balanced life. What areas of your life need evening out? Too much of one thing over another throws the rest off. Seek balance. Meditate on this and see what comes to mind for improvement.

Thoughts _____

_____

Application_____

_____

Other Verses_____

_____

THE PROFIT OF NOW

Proverbs 21:5 The plans of the diligent lead to
profit as surely as haste leads to poverty.

The beauty of diligence is the *profit* in outcomes. Rest assured that a well thought out plan is the source of many benefits. Be in that *profit* plan now. Know that the right direction and outcome will be orchestrated in time.

Thoughts _____

_____

Application_____

_____

Other Verses_____

_____

* * * * * * *

SELF-CONTROL OF NOW

Proverbs 24:28 Like a city whose walls are broken
through is a person who lacks *self-control*.

Self-control is a fruit of the Holy Spirit. You are far more able to enjoy *self-control* in the gentle peace of knowing that God is in control. Your main job is to keep your eye on the Lord for His nudging and direction. Breathe this in now.

Thoughts _____

_____

Application_____

_____

Other Verses_____

_____

THE HOLINESS OF NOW

Hebrews 12:14 Make every effort to live in peace with everyone
and to be holy; without *holiness*, no one will see the Lord.

The word *holiness* is very much related to wholeness. Being whole-
and complete is what is accomplished in your complete devotion
to God. Just to meditate on this concept of *holiness* brings you to
a complete state of reverence and peace. It is in this very moment
that *holiness* is brought to mind and expressed in your physical
being. Enjoy what it takes to be holy, a life in Christ.

Thoughts _____

_____

Application_____

_____

Other Verses_____

_____

* * * * * * *

THE EXULTATION OF NOW

1 Thessalonians 2:19 For who is our hope or joy or crown of
exultation? Is it not even you, in the presence of our Lord Jesus at
His coming?

There is a joy of enthusiasm when you think of the crown of *exultation* to come. You who in this moment know that the best is yet
to be presented. Whatever is happening now around you cannot
compete in this moment with what God has promised to His people. Breathe in and know… that promise is yours now.

Thoughts _____

_____

Application_____

_____

Other Verses_____

_____

THE ADVENT OF NOW

Psalm 19:5 Which is as a bridegroom coming out of his
chamber; It rejoices as a strong man to run his course.

The *advent* of now can be celebrated in a knowing that Christ, the
Bridegroom, will be returning to claim His long awaited Bride, the
church. That anticipation is a reminder of the heavenly joy that
awaits you and can be enjoyed now as you live in His *advent*.

Thoughts _____

_____

Application_____

_____

Other Verses_____

_____

* * * * * * *

THE SOVEREIGNTY OF NOW

Psalm 103:19 The LORD has established His throne in the
heavens, And His *sovereignty* rules over all.

The *sovereignty* of now assures you that all injustices will be resolved
in God's time. He has already poised Himself to fight your battles
such to ensure that the unjust self-destruct. Relax and release all
injustice to your *sovereign* Lord.

Thoughts _____

_____

Application_____

_____

Other Verses_____

_____

THE PURITY OF NOW

1Timothy 4:12 Let no one look down on your youthfulness,
but rather in speech, conduct, love, faith and *purity*, show
yourself an example of those who believe.

The *purity* of now is the righteous faith in your Lord as the example
of complete holiness. You are His and have that *purity* of intention
available in the now. Live that purity this moment with complete
unity of mind in Christ.

Thoughts _____

_____

Application_____

_____

Other Verses_____

_____

* * * * * * *

THE ABUNDANCE OF NOW

2Corinthians 9:8 And God is able to make all grace abound
to you, so that always having all sufficiency in everything, you
may have an *abundance* for every good deed.

Everything that you need is available right now. Take that thought
with you all day long. Wherever you look, God has been there with
His *abundance*. Breathe in and enjoy the *abundance* of now.

Thoughts _____

_____

Application_____

_____

Other Verses_____

_____

THE STEADFASTNESS OF NOW

2 Thessalonians 3:5 May the Lord direct your hearts into the
love of God and into the *steadfastness* of Christ.

There is a reward to the *steadfastness* of now. The faith of persistence, determination and even stubbornness has its own reward. Take this word of *steadfastness* with you all day long. See how it changes things for you now.

Thoughts _____

_____

Application_____

_____

Other Verses_____

_____

* * * * * * *

THE SUFFICIENCY OF NOW

2 Corinthians 12:9 And He has said to me, "My grace is *sufficient*
for you, for power is perfected in weakness." Most gladly,
therefore, I will rather boast about my weaknesses, so that the
power of Christ may dwell in me.

You have the benefit of God's grace, which allows for your *sufficiency*. You do not have to win favor for that grace. You can simply graciously receive it. Keep the *sufficiency* of now with you all day long.

Thoughts _____

_____

Application_____

_____

Other Verses_____

_____

THE RETURN OF NOW

1Peter 3:9 Not *returning* evil for evil or insult for insult, but giving a blessing instead; for you were called for the very purpose that you might inherit a blessing.

There are so many opportunities for *returning* a *blessing* in the now. God wins through love and you can too. Your words of God will not *return* void as it says in Isaiah 55:11. This is a powerful practice, as God wants us all to *return* to Him now.

Thoughts _____

_____

Application_____

_____

Other Verses_____

_____

* * * * * * *

THE OBSERVANCE OF NOW

Luke 11:28 But He said, "On the contrary, blessed are those who hear the word of God and *observe* it."

The word of God is so encouraging and uplifting. Those who study it are filled with the promise of hope. Yet, has worry been completely released? How does your life demonstrate the *observance* that no matter what happens, you are His?

Thoughts _____

_____

Application_____

_____

Other Verses_____

_____

THE ACTING OF NOW

Matthew 7:24 "Therefore everyone who hears these words
of Mine and *acts* on them, may be compared to a wise
man who built his house on the rock."

Focus on the *act* of now. In the quiet beat of your heart and the
joy of each breath, know that you are His. Nothing else can replace
what the presence of God in your life has to offer. *Act* now as the
Child of God that you are.

Thoughts _____

_____

Application_____

_____

Other Verses_____

_____

* * * * * * *

THE OPPORTUNITY OF NOW

Galatians 6:10 So then, while we have *opportunity*, let us
do good to all people, and especially to those who are of
the household of the faith.

Each moment of now is an *opportunity* to experience the presence
of the promise Jesus was brought to earth to give. Keeping that
glorious *opportunity* in mind, enjoy that fullness of joy now.

Thoughts _____

_____

Application_____

_____

Other Verses_____

_____

THE PERFORMANCE OF NOW

Hebrews 12:1 Therefore, since we have so great a cloud of witnesses surrounding us, let us also lay aside every encumbrance and the sin which so easily entangles us, and let us *run* with endurance the race that is set before us

You are running a race as with *performance*. Not in competition with anyone, but with yourself. You know the truth of what must be done and you do it in earnest with God's grace. Focusing now on the *performance* of faith demonstrated by those who have gone before you, breathe in the *run* of truth.

Thoughts _____

_____

Application_____

_____

Other Verses_____

_____

* * * * * * *

THE EXAMPLE OF NOW

1 Timothy 1:16 Yet for this reason I found mercy, so that in me as the foremost, Jesus Christ might demonstrate His perfect patience as an *example* for those who would believe in Him for eternal life.

In the *now*, you are an example of holiness and truth as a child of God. That example will carry you through each day as you live in your inheritance, with Creator and righteousness through Christ. Breathe in the example and live it.

Thoughts _____

_____

Application_____

_____

Other Verses_____

_____

THE APPLE OF NOW

Proverbs 7:2 Keep my commandments and live,
And my teaching as the *apple* of your eye.

What you focus on grows. As the *apple* of your eye becomes the teachings for your soul, God's commandments will emerge as the sweet taste of a fruitful life. Breathe in the commandments of God as the guide for daily living in blessings.

Thoughts _____

_____

Application_____

_____

Other Verses_____

_____

* * * * * * *

THE WILL OF NOW

John 2:19 Jesus answered them, "Destroy this
temple, and in three days I *will* raise it up."

The *will* is the voice of intention and prophecy. It stems from the intention of the present towards the future. Jesus demonstrated His prophecy of being raised up. Your *will* of now is the opportunity for you to live up to it. *Will* carefully.

Thoughts _____

_____

Application_____

_____

Other Verses_____

_____

THE SEED OF NOW

Matthew 13:31 He presented another parable to them, saying, "The kingdom of heaven is like a mustard *seed*, which a man took and sowed in his field…"

The *seed* of now is the tiniest beginning of something bigger than you can imagine. That *seed* is a thought that may grow to a tangible reality of experience. Know that your seed of thought, doubt, or other impression will grow to fruition. Plant the best *seeds* now.

Thoughts _____

_____

Application_____

_____

Other Verses_____

_____

* * * * * * *

THE KINGDOM OF NOW

Colossians 1:13 For He rescued us from the domain of darkness, and transferred us to the *kingdom* of His beloved Son.

The *kingdom* of now is the life of everlasting light, love and wisdom in Christ Jesus. You are a child of the King living in His *kingdom* and to His good pleasure for eternal fellowship and joy. Celebrate that *kingdom* now in anticipation. Participate in the victory of Christ now.

Thoughts _____

_____

Application_____

_____

Other Verses_____

_____

THE SEEKING OF NOW

1 Chronicles 22:19 Now devote your heart and soul
to seeking the Lord your God.

The treasures in store for those who *seek* the Lord are immeasurable. Rest in the knowing that you will see Him as He is and that He is there for you. Just contemplate the *seeking* of God now as you trust in His presence with you.

Thoughts _____

_____

Application_____

_____

Other Verses_____

_____

* * * * * * *

THE _____ OF NOW

(Create your own NOW experience)

Your Chosen Verse

Thoughts _____

_____

Application_____

_____

Other Verses_____

_____

THE _____ OF NOW

(Create your own NOW experience)

Your Chosen Verse

Thoughts _____

_____

Application_____

_____

Other Verses_____

_____

* * * * * * *

THE _____ OF NOW

(Create your own NOW experience)

Your Chosen Verse

Thoughts _____

_____

Application_____

_____

Other Verses_____

_____

THE _____ **OF NOW**

(Create your own NOW experience)

Your Chosen Verse

Thoughts _____

_____

Application_____

_____

Other Verses_____

_____

* * * * * * *

THE _____ **OF NOW**

(Create your own NOW experience)

Your Chosen Verse

Thoughts _____

_____

Application_____

_____

Other Verses_____

_____

THE _____ OF NOW

(Create your own NOW experience)

Your Chosen Verse

Thoughts _____

_____

Application_____

_____

Other Verses_____

_____

* * * * * * *

THE _____ OF NOW

(Create your own NOW experience)

Your Chosen Verse

Thoughts _____

_____

Application_____

_____

Other Verses_____

_____

Summary Comments

As you prepare for your future in eternity, know that God, the Father, God, the Son and God, the Holy Spirit, is with you *now*. You can carry the wisdom of these verses with you as you experience His presence all day long.

Now has so many attributes, I would imagine that you have additional ones of your own to add to this list. As you continue to experience the reality of *now* with complete engagement and with its many facets, you will begin to grow more fully into the reality of God.

You will become the vehicle of His love and creativity. You will live in joy, clarity of truth and productivity as you become more fruitful and multiply. You will find yourself creating your joy as a human being instead of a human doing *now*. Your life *now* is the dictate for your eternity. Choose well.

43753080R00099

Made in the USA
San Bernardino, CA
26 December 2016